FREE MASK

You Will Need:

- Thin elastic, wool or string

- Scissors

- Sticky Tape

Instructions:

1. Pull out the mask page.
2. Pop out the mask.
3. Cut enough elastic/wool/string to fit around the back of your head.
4. Attach to the back of the mask with some sticky tape.
5. Have fun with your new mask!

SCISSORS ARE SHARP! ASK AN ADULT FOR HELP BEFORE USING.

CONTENTS

Pedigree®

Published 2013. Pedigree Books Limited, Beech Hill House, Walnut Gardens, Exeter, Devon EX4 4DH. www.pedigreebooks.com – books@pedigreegroup.co.uk The Pedigree trademark, email and website addresses, are the sole and exclusive properties of Pedigree Group Limited, used under licence in this publication.

WELCOME

TO THE WORLD OF

It's time to head to Quahog, Rhode Island, home of the Griffins. They're not your normal family as father Peter is officially retarded, mom Lois is a reformed kleptomaniac, daughter Meg once got caught up in an ear sex craze, son Chris had a monkey living in his closet and baby Stewie invented his own time machine. Oh, and they have a talking dog called Brian! With sex-crazed Glenn Quagmire and wheelchair using cop Joe Swanson as neighbours, Quahog is a crazy place to be. So come with us as we head into the madcap lives of the Griffins.

We take a look at all the episodes of the latest season of the show, along with games, quizzes, looks at Family Guy over the years and loads more!

The GRIFFIN Family

PETER GRIFFIN

The patriarch of the Griffin clan, Peter didn't have the greatest start in life. He was born in Mexico, where his mother had gone to abort him, which meant that he didn't officially become a US citizen until he was in his 40s. While he grew up thinking the strict, critical and very Catholic Francis was his father, he later discovered he was actually the result of his mother's brief dalliance with drunken Irishman Mickey McFinnigan.

He's certainly not the smartest cookie, as an IQ test revealed that he's officially classed as mentally retarded. Luckily for him though, Lois didn't mind about the low intelligence of the young man she met while he was working as a towel boy for her Aunt Marguerite. They married and now have three children, who all have to deal with his mad shenanigans, which range from going blind after trying to break the record for eating the most nickels to making a chick flick called Steel Vaginas.

A MAN OF MANY JOBS

While Family Guy has been on the air, Peter has had three main jobs – he started off working in a toy factory, then became a fisherman, before he landed a job in the shipping department of the Pawtucket Brewery. However, in various episodes and cutaways, it's been revealed Peter has had an awful lot of professions in his time. Here are just some of them.

- Towel boy
- Bathroom attendant
- Transvestite prostitute
- Renaissance fair jouster
- Sneeze guard
- President of his own country
- Death substitute
- The Green Guy in Tron
- Butt scratcher seller
- Channel 5 News 'Grind My Gears' special reporter
- Sheriff of Bumblescum
- CEO of Pewterschmidt Industries
- Vice President of the El Dorado Cigarette Company
- Matt Damon's neck

- Night-time heat provider for Lara Flynn Boyle
- Uma Thurman's eye wrangler
- Professional American Football player
- Sumo wrestler
- Erotic book author
- Restaurant owner
- Television producer
- Preacher
- Airline pilot
- Policeman
- Servant
- Calvin Klein Model
- George Harrison's security guard
- Christina Aguilera's manager
- Bulimia clinic counsellor
- Construction worker
- Fast food cashier
- Cocoa Puffs mascot
- Superstore USA employee
- School board president
- Undercover drug investigator
- Sandy Duncan's glass eye
- Robin William's starting point for his jokes

TOP 05 PETER QUOTES

PETER: Hey, excuse me, is your refrigerator running, because if it is, it probably runs like you... very homosexually.
From: Lethal Weapons

PETER: You know. I always thought that dogs laid eggs. And today I learned something
From: Screwed The Pooch

PETER: Lois, before I found these movies, women only made me cry through my penis. Now they make me cry through my eyes.
From: Chick Cancer

LOIS: Peter, you're bribing your daughter with a car?
PETER: Come on, Lois, isn't 'bribe' just another word for love?
From: I Never Met The Dead Man

PETER: Holy crip, he's a crapple.
From: A Hero Sits Next Door

FAMILY GUY FACT
In the episode 'Wasted Talent' we learn that Peter can play the piano – but only when he's drunk.

The GRIFFIN Family

LOIS GRIFFIN

Lois Griffin may look like the all-American mother on the outside, but she certainly has an unusual past. She's the daughter of the fabulously wealthy industrialist Carter Pewterschmidt and his wife Barbara. Lois grew up surrounded by money and privilege, although her family could be rather distant – as shown when they refused to even consider paying a ransom when she was kidnapped as a teenager.

This resulted in Lois becoming a bit rebellious and getting a reputation for sleeping around. When she met Peter, she left her life of privilege behind to settle down in the lower middle class income bracket and raise a family. However, her tendency to go to the extreme is never far under the surface, whether it's becoming a kleptomaniac or indulging in S&M sex. It's little wonder that she sometimes feels the need to act out, as she constantly has to deal with the madcap and often destructive tendencies of her husband, who constantly tests her patience.

TOP 05 LOIS QUOTES

LOIS: Joe, you're too heavy. I can't hang on!
JOE: Pretend I'm your child, Lois! [She starts to drop him]
JOE: NOT MEG! NOT MEG!
From: Breaking Out Is Hard To Do

MEG: Mom, is sodomy illegal if you're Jewish?
LOIS: I hope so, Meg. I really do.
From: Family Goy

LOIS: Look, Stewie, a note. You know, Mommy doesn't usually read things out of Chris' pocket. She's more respectful than that.
STEWIE: Yeah, whatever helps you sleep at night, bitch.
From: Fast Times At Buddy Cianci Jr. High

LOIS: Oh, I haven't been on a college campus in years. Everything seems so different.
STEWIE: Really? Perhaps if you laid on your back with your ankles behind your ears that would ring a few bells.
From: The Story On Page One

LOIS: [talking about Peter] This is a man who thinks the plural of goose is sheep.
From: Running Mates

LOOSE LOIS

Lois' public persona as a homemaker and piano teacher hides a far kinkier side. Throughout the series we've seen hints at the sexual extremes she enjoys and that in her youth she wasn't afraid to put out.

Before she married Peter she had the nickname 'Loose Lois', as revealed by Gene Simmons of the rock band KISS, who slept with her in the 1980s. Indeed she was so well known back then that he's told the other band members of her legendary exploits. She was a bit of a groupie back then, sleeping with various rock stars and their entourages (including making a plaster cast of singer Daryl Hall's genitals), as well as starring in a pornographic movie.

It's also been suggested that Lois may have had a few dalliances with ladies in the past, such as saying in the episode 'Stewie B. Good', "Women are such teases. that's why I went back to men." She's admitted to practicing kissing with her female friends as a teen and had to be told by Joe's wife Bonnie not to rub

sunscreen so low and erotically on her back.

We've seen her engaging in leather-bound S&M sex with Peter (the safety word is Banana), enjoying having a cigarette put out on her, asking Peter to put his finger in a bullet hole and twist it after she was shot and wanting to be kicked in the breasts! She's even forced Peter to have sex, but thinks this is okay because she believes that women can't rape men!

Lois also wants to pass down her proclivities to her daughter Meg, giving her some unusual sex advice.

HERE IT IS:

LOIS: Look Meg – A: Ear sex is just unnatural, and B: How do I say this, vaginal intercourse is... it's just tops! It's the bee's knees, Meg. Oh, when you rattle it around just right, oh my god! I mean, you

remember when we had that old car with the bad shocks, and I used to take the old dirt road on purpose! Meg! Meg?
From: Prick Up Your Ears

LOIS: You don't have enough passion. Sometimes a woman wants to see a man be a man. You gotta push back a little. You gotta get a little rough! Oh God, Peter hit me!
From: The Loretta-Cleveland Quagmire

LOIS: The Army are weak, the Marines now they are the guys you want to f**k.
From: Saving Private Brian

The GRIFFIN Family

MEG GRIFFIN

It's not easy being the beanie-hat wearing Meg. The Griffin's 18-year-old daughter has to put up with her family's constant disapproval, with Peter often telling her to shut up, Lois laughing at the idea she might have a social life and Chris teasing her. Even when someone does show some interest – such as Brian kissing her at a high school dance – it turns out the dog only did it because he was drunk.

However, her role as the family kicking post may be necessary, as when she fought back in the episode 'Seahorse Seashell Party', the whole family started to disintegrate. As she put it, "Do you think it's possible that this family can't survive without some sort of lightning rod to absorb all the dysfunction? Maybe if I feel bad, they don't have to." As a result she decided to accept her role as the family punching bag. Thankfully the other Griffins do sometimes show they care, such as Brian and Stewie rescuing her when she was kidnapped during a trip to Europe.

SHUT UP MEG!

FAMILY GUY FACT
In 'Stewie Griffin: The Untold Story' it's suggested Meg will eventually become a transsexual man called Ron.

MEG'S DIARY

While she has to spend much of her life bearing the ridicule of her family and just about everyone she meets – as well as sometimes fending off the sexual advances of next door neighbour Glenn Quagmire – Meg does find solace writing in her diary.

Although we've only ever gotten to hear snippets of what Meg writes, it's where she pours out all her feelings. Indeed, if she ever did want to take her family to court, it would be her best evidence!

From her thoughts about boys to her feelings about growing up, it all goes in there. Writing things down can be a double-edged sword though, as while it might make her feel better, her family do like to have a laugh by reading it.

Here are a few snippets from the secret tome:

"DEAR DIARY, STILL NO SIGN OF THAT TAMPON FROM LAST WEEK, BUT THE HEADACHES ARE GETTING WORSE."
From: Brian Griffin's House Of Payne

(LOIS READING MEG'S DIARY WITH THE REST OF THE FAMILY GATHERED AROUND)
LOIS: DEAR DIARY, KEVIN IS SO HOT. TODAY HE WAS RAKING THE YARD. GOD I WISH HE'D THROW ME INTO THAT PILE OF LEAVES. [EVERYONE LAUGHS]
MEG: HEY WHAT'S EVERYONE...OH MY GOD! YOU'RE READING MY DIARY! I HATE YOU ALL! [SHE RUNS AWAY]
PETER: KEEP GOING.
From: Stuck Together Torn Apart

MEG: DEAR DIARY. TODAY AT THE SCHOOL LIBRARY I SAW A PICTURE IN NATIONAL GEOGRAPHIC OF A WOMAN WITH NIPPLES THAT COVER MOST OF HER BREAST TOO, AND SUDDENLY I DIDN'T FEEL SO ALONE.
From: The Man With Two Brians

TOP 05 MEG QUOTES

MEG: I got a makeover, dad. Don't I look great?
PETER: Oh, Meg, honey, I always thought you looked beautiful just the way...
[breaks into laughter] Couldn't do that with a straight face!
From: Don't Make Me Over

BRIAN: Hey Meg! Listen, I hope you feel alright about our talk the other day. You know, about us being just friends and all.
MEG: Oh, yeah, no. I'm fine, I'm fine. And hey, I wanted to thank you for being so great to me, so I baked you a pie.

BRIAN: Oh wow. Hey that looks delicious. Mmm, oh, this is good. What's in there?
MEG: Well, there's some apples and some cinnamon... and my hair.
From: Barely Legal

CHRIS: [After learning they have a black ancestor] Cool, I get to be black and Irish.
MEG: Yeah, and now I can wear clothes that actually show off my big butt.
From: Peter Griffin - Husband, Father... Brother?

LOIS: Oh look, Meg, it's your little baby booties, and your little bronzed hat, and your tail.
MEG: My what?
LOIS: Nothing.
From: Fore Father

CHRIS GRIFFIN

Like his dad, Chris isn't the cleverest of people, but he's a fairly typical teenage boy who spends his time watching movies, thinking about girls, hanging out with his friends, and masturbating – the latter of which he does so frequently that at one point Lois even wondered whether cleaning Chris' sheets had made the washing machine pregnant.

He may seem dim but he does have hidden talents. His skill at art resulted in him briefly becoming a painting sensation known as Christobel, and when the Griffins moved to England, he was almost immediately able to pick up Cockney slang. It's a miracle he's as coherent as he is, as Lois has admitted drinking and smoking a lot while she was pregnant with him, as she was hoping to induce a miscarriage. Then, when he was born, he was so enormous a newspaper article dubbed him an 'Elephant Child'. Chris is often a little self-conscious about his weight, but he does have something that makes his father extremely jealous – a large penis.

TOP 05 CHRIS QUOTES

CHRIS: I never knew anyone who went crazy before, except for my imaginary friend Captain Sprock!
From: I Never Met The Dead Man

HERBERT: Selling your old hand-me-downs?
CHRIS: Yep.
HERBERT: You got anything that you used to wear in the summertime?
CHRIS: Just these old shorts.
HERBERT: Sweet Jesus.
From: Road to Rupert

CHRIS: My dad's smarter than your dad.
PETER: We have the same dad, idiot!
CHRIS: Yeah, but mine's smarter!
From: Petarded

CHRIS: You're a dog! You don't have a soul!
BRIAN: Ouch.
From: North By North Quahog

CHRIS: I was going to school, but this guy won't let me.
PETER: Oh yeah? Him and what army?
CHRIS: The US Army.
From: E Peterbus Unum

FAMILY GUY FACT
Chris' birthday is February 8th, the same as Seth Green, the actor who plays his voice.

Chris Griffin isn't just a bit dim, he's also incredibly impressionable. You can convince him to do just about anything if you promise him the outcome will be good. Here are just a few examples...

CHRIS THE JEW
In the episode When You Wish Upon a Weinstein, Peter becomes convinced that the only way for Chris to become smart and successful is for his son to become a Jew. While Lois is dead set against it (she didn't know at the time her own mother was a Jewish Holocaust survivor), Peter and Chris are determined, heading off to Las Vegas to get a quickie Bar Mitzvah. However, Lois arrives just in time to stop it.

CHRIS THE REPUBLICAN
Most of the time Chris isn't very interested in politics, but in the episode 'You May Now Kiss the...Uh...Guy Who Receives' he becomes a be-suited, straight-laced Young Republican. While Brian is putting together a petition to get Quahog to legalise gay marriage, Chris is convinced by his fellow Republicans to destroy it. However, Chris isn't doing this out of a real belief in conservative values, it's simply because another Young Republican called Alyssa has told him he can touch her boobs if he does what she says.

CHRIS THE ROCKER
In the episode 'Saving Private Brian', Chris hasn't shown much interest in rock music until his father introduces him to a metal band at his school. Chris takes to the Goth lifestyle immediately, becoming a hit with the band Splash Log at a school dance (where he sings about the monkey in his closet). He also picks up an extremely antisocial attitude, being rude to his parents and all those around him. Peter and Lois end up having to recruit Marilyn Manson – who they initially blame for Chris becoming unpleasant – to come and tell Chris he can like the music and be a responsible citizen too.

CHRIS THE RUNAWAY
You can understand that Chris wouldn't want to be paddled with a bat by older students on his first day at High School (which is a Quahog tradition), but the eldest Griffin son takes things to the extreme. Barely minutes after Brian has told Chris about the existence of the Peace Corps, Chris has signed up and run away to South America. It doesn't go well though, with Chris accidentally getting married in a jungle village. When his family turn up, he agrees to go back to Quahog with them.

STEWIE GRIFFIN

For a one-year-old, Stewie is certainly smart. In fact he's clever for any age, having managed to invent everything from a time machine to a contraption that allows him to traverse the multiverse. Early on in his life he used his brains to plot against his mother, planning all manner of terrible ends for her. More recently his villainous side has softened, although that doesn't mean he can't bring out the big guns if he needs to battle an enemy, such as his half-brother Bertram. Stewie's also suggested he's left a time bomb in Lois' womb that will go off on her 50th birthday!

While most family members seem to only understand Stewie intermittently, Brian always knows what the baby is talking about, and he's undoubtedly Stewie's closest friend. While the baby and dog often have a tempestuous relationship – Stewie once beat Brian up and shot him in the kneecaps over a debt – the baby has admitted how much he loves the dog. They often end up on adventures together, whether it's to Nazi Germany or heading across the US to retrieve Stewie's lost teddy bear Rupert.

STEWIE'S INVENTIONS

The world has never seen a genius like Stewie Griffin, who is able to invent things that have baffled even the greatest of scientists - and he's only one-year-old! Here are some of the incredible contraptions he's come up with:

- Laser pistol
- Mind control device
- Weather control device
- Gun that freezes people in carbonite
- Mass hypnosis machine
- Robot versions of Peter, Brian, himself and other people
- Miniaturisation device ship capable of being injected into Peter's bloodstream
- Time machine
- Matter transporter
- Multiverse-traversing controller
- Machine that can immerse you in a false world to show you how your decisions will turn out
- Cloning technology
- Rocket skis complete with small house to have tea in
- Hovering drill
- Stealth bomber jets
- Body switching orb
- The Big Bang – which he accidentally sets off when his time machine sends himself and Brian outside of time and space

TOP 05 STEWIE QUOTES

CHRIS: Hey, birthday dude! You want some ice cream?
STEWIE: Yes, but no sprinkles. For every sprinkle I find, I shall kill you.
From: Chitty Chitty Death Bang

STEWIE: Women, Brian, what a royal pain in the ass. It's like, it's like why can't you just hang out with guys, you know, just live with someone of your own sex, just do what you do with women, but with your buddy. You know what, why don't guys just do that?
BRIAN: They do...
It's called being gay.
STEWIE: Oh, is that what gay is? Oh, yeah. I could totally get into that.
From: Chick Cancer

STEWIE: Come on, discipline me! Make me wear panties, rub dirt in my eye, violate me with a wine bottle. My God, I really do have problems, don't I?
From: Peter's Two Dads

DYLAN: Stewie, why are you nude?
STEWIE: Oh, just a little something I do once a week around here called a 'naked tea party'. Got my teacup here and now all I need is a teabag. That something that might interest you, my friend?
From: The Former Life Of Brian

STEWIE: [wearing drag] None for me, thanks. It's gonna go straight to my vagina. That's what girls worry about, right? Having big vaginas?
From: Boys Do Cry

FAMILY GUY FACT
In early Family Guy episodes Stewie often said he wanted to kill Lois. However, in the episode 'And Then There Were Fewer' he saves her from being murdered by news anchor Diane Simmons.

BRIAN GRIFFIN

Brian is a white Labrador who's been a member of the Griffin household ever since Peter invited him to stay after finding him begging on the streets. Oh, and he can talk, which doesn't seem that unusual to anyone in Quahog. Brian doesn't originate from Rhode Island though, as he was born on a puppy farm in Texas – and was horrified when he returned to discover his mother had been stuffed and turned into an end table!

When he's not running scared of the vacuum or sniffing other dog's butts, he thinks of himself as highly cultured, with a love of opera, art and a desire to be a great writer. Sadly for him when his debut novel, Faster Than The Speed Of Love, was published, it hardly sold any copies. However, he did later find success with a self-help book that he wrote, even though he knew everything contained in it was rubbish. The rest of the Griffins aren't sure Brian is as cultured and smart as he pretends, particularly as he has a tendency to date stupid women he picks purely on their looks. It would probably also help if he didn't drink as much.

FASTER THAN THE SPEED OF LOVE BC

BEWARE OF DOG!

FAMILY GUY FACT
While Family Guy creator Seth McFarlane voices Brian, he's said that when the show was originally being developed, Oscar-nominated actor William H. Macy auditioned for the role.

TOP 05 BRIAN QUOTES

STEWIE: [imitating Brian] I'm the dog! I'm well-read and have a diverse stock portfolio. But I'm not above eating grass clippings and regurgitating them on the small braided rug near the door!
BRIAN: [imitating Stewie] I'm a pompous little Antichrist who will probably abandon my plans for world domination when I grow up and fall in love with a rough trick named Jim.
From: Lethal Weapons

WOMAN IN BAR: I think you've had enough to drink
BRIAN: I think you're wrong you increasingly attractive looking woman. You could be in magazines. You could. And not just Jugs or Creamsicle.
From: Road To Rhode Island

BRIAN: [to Meg] If there was a God, would he give you a smoking hot mom like Lois and then have you grow up looking like Peter?
From: Not All Dogs Go To Heaven

STEWIE: How can you have a 13-year-old son when you're only 7?
BRIAN: Those are dog years.

STEWIE: That doesn't make any sense.
BRIAN: You know what, Stewie? If you don't like it, go on the internet and complain.
From: The Former Life Of Brian

BRIAN: [looking at the toilet] How do you think it works?
STEWIE: I have no idea.
BRIAN: Look, Lois told me I had to start using the toilet and you're the one who's had potty training, so I'm counting on you to help me...
STEWIE: All right, we're two intelligent guys. We can figure this out. *From: Bill & Peter's Bogus Journey*

BRIAN VS. QUAGMIRE

Brian thinks he's got pretty much everyone, including himself, convinced he's a wonderful, highly cultured and artistic pooch. However, there's one person who remains resolutely unimpressed – Glenn Quagmire. The sex hound neighbour of the Griffins can't stand the dog, and in the episode Jerome Is The New Black he unloads and let's Brian know exactly what he thinks of him.

Is Glenn right about Brian, or is he being unfair? Here's what Glenn had to say:

BRIAN: How can you not like me?
QUAGMIRE: Okay, I'll tell you. You are the worst person I know. You constantly hit on your best friend's wife. The man pays for your food and rescued you from certain death, and this is how you repay him? And to add insult to injury, you defecate all over his yard. And you're such a sponge. You pay for nothing. You always say, "Oh, I'll get you later", but later never comes!

And what really bothers me is you pretend you're this deep guy who

loves women for their souls when all you do is date bimbos. Yeah, I date women for their bodies but at least I'm honest about it. I don't buy them a copy of Catcher in the Rye and then lecture them with some seventh grade interpretation of how Holden Caulfield is some profound, intellectual. He wasn't, he was a spoiled brat. And that's why you like him so much – he's you! God, you're pretentious. And you delude yourself by thinking you're some great writer, even though you're terrible.

You know, I should have known Cheryl Tiegs didn't write me that note. She would have known there's no 'a' in the word 'definite'. And I think what I hate most about you is your textbook liberal agenda, how we should 'legalize pot, man'. How big business is crushing the underclass. How homelessness is the biggest tragedy in America. Well, what have YOU done to help? I work down at the soup kitchen, Brian. Never seen you down there. You wanna help? Grab a ladle!

And by the way, driving a Prius

doesn't make you Jesus Christ! Oh, wait, you don't believe in Jesus Christ or any religion for that matter, because 'religion is for idiots'. Well, who the hell are you to talk down to anyone? You failed college twice, which isn't nearly as bad as your failure as a father. How's that son of yours you never see? But you know what? I could forgive all of that, all of it, if you weren't such a bore. That's the worst of it, Brian. You're just a big, sad, alcoholic bore.

Well, see ya, Brian.
Thanks for the BLEEPing steak!

GLENN QUAGMIRE

It's safe to say that few people on this planet like sex as much as Glenn Quagmire. All day, every day, Glenn is either thinking about or having sex. His house is specially adapted so that it can go from normal suburban pad to pleasure palace at the touch of a button. He's such a sex hound that not even his long friendship with Peter could stop him from hitting on Meg the moment she turned 18. However, if there was one woman he would have above all others (except perhaps model Cheryl Tiegs) it would probably be Lois. His attraction to her is slightly unhealthy though, as he's gone as far as to build a model of her he keeps in his closet, made out of things she's thrown away in the trash. It was a shame for Glenn that Peter came along, as in an alternate timeline where Lois never married Peter, she got together with Quagmire instead.

Glenn does find time to do a few other things than having sex. To pay for his pleasures he works as an airline pilot. He can often be found drinking with Peter and Joe at the Drunken Clam. And perhaps unexpectedly Quagmire has a weakness for cats, often boring people to tears with his mushy adoration of every cute little thing a feline does.

TOP 05 QUAGMIRE QUOTES

PETER: [shouting out of the window] Hey, everybody! Meg just had her first period!
JOE: Peter, shut up! It's 3:00 in the morning!
CLEVELAND: What the hell is going on out there?
QUAGMIRE: Damn it! People are trying to sleep!
PETER: I'm just saying, I'm proud of her! She's a woman! Yeah!
QUAGMIRE: Yes, Peter, that's very hot, and I'll deal with it in the morning, but right now, I'm exhausted! *From: Model Misbehaviour*

QUAGMIRE: We know you have your choice in airport sex, and we thank you for choosing Quagmire. Please exercise caution when standing up, as the contents in your vagina may have shifted during coitus. *From: Airport '07*

PETER: How am I gonna come up with 50 grand by tomorrow?
QUAGMIRE: Well, you could whore yourself out to a thousand fat chicks for 50 bucks apiece, or 50 really fat chicks for a thousand bucks. What? Don't look at me like that. Fat chicks need love too, but they gotta pay! *From: A Fish Out Of Water*

QUAGMIRE: I gotta find a way out of this marriage. Cleveland, how did you get out of yours?
CLEVELAND: You slept with my wife. *From: I Take Thee, Quagmire*

QUAGMIRE: I felt guilty once, but she woke up halfway through. *From: One If By Clam, Two If By Sea*

The Neighbours

JOE SWANSON

Not even being paralysed from the waist down can stop Joe Swanson from being a no-nonsense cop who'll take down any bad guy who gets in his way. He's an extremely macho, proud man who has a tendency to get extremely angry if he thinks anyone is mocking or teasing him. For years he told anyone who asked that he was paralysed while trying to prevent a Grinch-like creature from ruining Christmas, but as we discover in the latest season, that's not the real truth.

Joe is married to Bonnie and has a young daughter called Susie (born after a lengthy pregnancy that lasted from Season 1 to Season 7!). They also have a son called Kevin who Joe believed had been killed in Iraq. It turned out that Kevin had used an explosion to hide the fact that he was going AWOL. He eventually decided to return home to Spooner Street, and while Joe initially felt he ought to take his kid to jail, he decided to keep his son's secret and allow Kevin to stay out of the brig. That mercy doesn't stretch to others who break the law though, as they'd better watch out for the all-action Joe!

TOP 05 JOE QUOTES

JOE: Hey Peter, what's up?
PETER: Joe, I just recently found out that I'm, umm, I'm mentally retarded, and I just wanted to ask – how do you deal with it?
JOE: Peter, I'm handicapped, not retarded.
PETER: Okay, now we're splitting hairs. *From: Petarded*

CLEVELAND: [while bowling] I must say, I do feel a strange satisfaction watching the black ball topple all those self-righteous white pins.
JOE: Can't blame them for being self-righteous. The black ball's in their neighbourhood uninvited.
CLEVELAND: The black ball's done nothing wrong.
JOE: If the black ball's innocent, it has nothing to fear.
From: Blind Ambition

JOE: We've captured the burglars.
LOIS: Oh, thank God!
JOE: Unfortunately, they're pressing sexual harassment charges against your daughter.
From: Untitled Griffin Family History

[During Bonnie's labour]
DR. HARTMAN: Okay, Mrs. Swanson, you're almost there.
JOE: Get outta there! Get the hell outta my wife, you little bastard!
From: Ocean's Three And A Half

CHRIS: One time my dad pooped in the neighbour's yard and lied about it.
JOE: I knew it! Well, I'm glad I used his shovel to clean it up.
From: Fifteen Minutes Of Shame

The Neighbours...

MORT GOLDMAN

Pharmacist Mort Goldman is Family Guy's stereotypical Jew, with a nasal voice, thrifty attitude and tendency towards hypochondria. He's got a son called Neil, who used to spend a lot of time lusting after Meg. Sadly though his wife Muriel was murdered when news anchor Diane Simmons went on a killing spree. Indeed Mort rarely has much luck, as he's managed to accidentally travel back in time to Nazi Europe (just as Jews were being rounded up), and his pharmacy has been looted, robbed, burned to the ground and had a dead horse thrown through the window (by Peter).

MAYOR WEST

As you'd expect from such a crazy place as Quahog, its civic leader is an unusual bureaucrat. Mayor West is rather paranoid, such as worrying who's stealing his water (when it's simply going down the drain), and has no qualms about wasting taxpayers money, including erecting a solid gold statue of breakfast cereal cartoon character Dig 'Em frog and sending the town's entire police force to South America to rescue a fictional character from a 1980s movie. Despite his often peculiar behaviour, Lois' sister Carol fell in love with him and they married soon after her eighth divorce.

HERBERT

Friendly Local Pederast

Herbert may be a very old man, but that hasn't put him off his favourite hobby – trying to lure children and teenage boys into his clutches. Although most neighbourhoods would hate having a paedophile in their midst, Herbert is old, feeble and harmless-looking enough that he gets away with it. He drives around in an ice cream van, hatching plans to get close to boys – none of which ever succeed. He's long been interested in Chris, but never gets very far with him.

OTHER PEOPLE YOU MIGHT MEET AROUND QUAHOG:

CARTER & BARBARA PEWTERSCHMIDT

Lois' parents are fabulously rich, living in the lap of luxury in a gargantuan mansion. Carter owns U.S. Steel and Pewterschmidt Industries, and while he once tried to retire, he needs the energy of being a captain of industry to keep him going. He's brusque, hates the poor and has long loathed his son-in-law, Peter. Barbara meanwhile is a holocaust survivor who hid her Jewish heritage in order to join the wealthy, white, Christian world of rich New Englanders.

CONSUELA

Quahog Maid Services

The broken-englished Hispanic maid is unusual as she's one of the few characters from a cutaway gag to become a 'regular' in the series. We first saw her in a gag where she was head of the Maids' Unions, who demands more cleaning spray during a court case. Since then she's briefly been the Griffin's maid and has cleaned for various other characters too. Consuela also tried to keep Stewie after she found him on the street.

ANGELA – Peter's boss

OPIE – Peter's co-worker

FOUAD – Another of Peter's colleagues

BRUCE – Mustachioed and soft spoken master of many jobs

CARL – Convenience store manager who's Meg & Chris' sometime boss

CONNIE D'AMICO – Popular high school girl and Meg's enemy

DEATH – The Grim Reaper

DR. ELMER HARTMAN – The Griffin's regular physician

HORACE – Owner of The Drunken Clam bar

TOM TUCKER – Channel 5 Action News' male anchor

JAKE TUCKER – Tom Tucker's son who has an upside-down face

JOYCE KINNEY – Female news anchor who replaced the homicidal Diane Simmons

TRICIA TAKANAWA – Channel 5 News' Asian reporter

OLLIE WILLIAMS – Monosyllabic weatherman

JILLIAN – The dim-witted ex-love of Brian, who he still pines over

SEAMUS – Wooden armed & legged sea-dog

JASPER – Brian's gay cousin

BERTRAM – Stewie's half-brother, born via Peter's accidental sperm donation

PATRICK PEWTERSCHMIDT – Lois' brother, who was locked up for strangling fat guys (but has since escaped)

EVIL MONKEY – Pointing chimp who used to live in Chris' closet

THE GIANT CHICKEN – An oversized avian in an on-going feud with Peter

GREASED-UP DEAF GUY – The name says it all!

Quahog

History

Local legend says that Quahog was founded by Miles 'Chatterbox' Musket, who set out on a voyage to America many years ago. However, he annoyed those on the ship with his constant chattering, so they threw him overboard. He was saved from drowning by a talking clam, who took him to Rhode Island, and there they founded Quahog.

Sadly though, Miles and the clam eventually fell out (once more over Musket's endless blathering), and the clam left. Every year afterwards of that day, Miles went to the beach, hoping the clam would return, and in memory of that, the town holds a festival every year where they hope the same thing will happen.

Others say this is just a founding myth, and that Quahog was actually started by Griffin Petersen, after he was exiled to America by King Stewart III.

Things To Do...

THE DRUNKEN CLAM

If you fancy a quiet drink – don't go to The Drunken Clam. However, if you don't mind never knowing what might happen, head on down.

For many years the bar was run by landlord Horace, who's always on hand to serve the Pawtucket Brewery's finest brews. The Clam has been a Quahog landmark for decades. While it was briefly sold to Nigel Pinchley and turned into a British pub, Horace quickly bought it back and it returned to being the Drunken Clam.

While you're there you may run into Peter Griffin, who's not only a loyal customer but also a bit of a hero, having once saved Horace from a terrible fire. Sadly though, Horace recently died, putting the future of this Quahog landmark in doubt.

SCHOOLS

If you're thinking of settling in Quahog, there's a fine range of educational establishments. Your youngest ones can attend the Hugs and Kisses Day Care. For older kids there's Buddy Cianci Junior High School (named after a long-serving Providence mayor who was imprisoned for racketeering), and James Woods High School.

PETORIA

It may not exist anymore, but if you head to Spooner Street, you can see the site of one of the most unusual geographical anomalies in United States history. It was discovered a few years ago that the plot of 31 Spooner Street was accidentally left off the official maps, allowing the owner – once more Peter Griffin – to declare independence and become President of his own sovereign nation, Petoria.

Petoria lasted less than a week, as Peter abused his power and annexed his neighbour's pool. Angry that Petoria had dared broach its borders, the United States surrounded the micro-country and forced the Griffins to surrender and sign an agreement that 31 Spooner Street was now part of the US.

FAMILY GUY FACT!

A quahog is a type of edible clam!

QUAHOG AIRPORT

When you've had enough of Quahog, the city has its own international airport, where pilots such as Glenn Quagmire will be pleased to take you to a range of destinations.

TANNING BABY SCANDAL!

Talk About A Crispy Critter!

Tanning is on the lips of everyone in Quahog after it was discovered a local one-year-old had joined in the craze. Stewie Griffin of Spooner Street decided he liked to tan after his dog took him on an all-day golf game. Soon he had his own tanning machine and decided he loved the lifestyle. He even began holding parties only for tanned people.

However, things went wrong for Stewie when he went for a tan and relied on his dog to wake him up after fifteen minutes. Unfortunately Brian fell asleep and Stewie was in the bed for six and a half hours, ending up completely burnt from head to foot.

While he eventually began to peel, Stewie became convinced he had skin cancer and might die (although thankfully he was given the all clear). So all of you out there in Quahog, be careful of sun beds!

YOUNG QUAHOG INVENTOR DEVELOPS PHOTON RAYGUN

Quahog can hold its head high when it comes to making weapons of mass destruction, as young Stewie Griffin has invented his very own Photon Raygun. Now all the little man's enemies had better beware, as he's ready to lay waste to then.

Stewie hasn't forgotten about the planet though, saying,

"I'm only using organic plutonium now. Think globally; buy locally."

WANTED:

For General Mayhem and Disturbing the Peace

QUAHOG POLICE DEPT. 0485219

Quahog Classifieds:

Do you want to have sex? Are you any woman? **Call Glenn Quagmire. GIGGITY.**

For Sale: One Petercopter. Slightly broken and covered in Joe's lawn after crash.

In Memoriam: *Muriel Goldman* – Wife, mother and Jew. Her family misses her, especially how good she was at cheating her customers. **RIP.**

For Sale: Automaton Nuclear Neo-humanoid Android (A.N.N.A.) costume from Quahog Players production of *The King And I.*

For Sale: Painting by 10-minute art sensation *Christobel.*

The Quahog Beautiful People's Club is looking for members.

Ugly people need not apply.

Do you fear the Devil? Well, you should fear the Super-devil even more! Repent!

In Memoriam: Loretta Brown –

Mother and cheating wife. Died from having a brontosaurus skeleton dropped on her. **RIP.**

For Sale: S.S. More Powerful Than Superman, Batman, Spider-Man, and the Incredible Hulk Put Together fishing boat

THE BIG FAT FAMILY GUY QUIZ

How much do you know about the world of Family Guy? Find out with our quiz!

1. The very first episode of Family Guy premiered after which much-watched sporting event in the US?

2. And in what year did that premiere take place?

3. On which street do the Griffins live?

4. When neighbour Cleveland Brown left Quahog, to which state did he move?

5. What was the name of Cleveland's wife (who he divorced after she slept with Quagmire)?

6. What is Chris Griffin's middle name?

7. Peter once went undercover as a student at James Wood high school. What name did he use?

8. The Griffins discovered they had an African-American slave ancestor. What was his name?

9. When Peter is forced to take over Death's duties for a while, he is tasked to kill the cast of which late-90s & early 00s TV series?

10. Which of the Griffins briefly became Mayor of Quahog?

11. And which of them was School Board President for a while?

12. Peter once got his own segment on Channel 5 News, which was called, 'What Really Grinds My ?????'

13. When Brian joins the police, what job do they give him?

14. What was the name of the toy company Peter worked for in the early days of Family Guy?

15. And what was the name of Peter's boss at the toy company?

16. Complete the name of the Alabama town the Griffins move to when they're put in the FBI Witness Protection Program – Bumble????

17. What is the name of the nudist family the Griffins encounter when Meg starts dating their son, Jeff?

18. Peter Griffin once started up his own television station. What was it called?

19. Chris accidentally got married when he ran away to which continent?

20. Peter was once hired to play for which US-based American Football team?

21. And which European team did they sell him to?

22. Quagmire married a woman the Griffins won as a maid-for-a-day. What was her first name?

23. Peter once launched a range of erotic books under which name?

24. When Brian got his own radio program, what was it called after Stewie joined him as co-host?

25. To what country does Peter travel to in order to find his biological father?

26. Which former US President did Lois once cheat on Peter with?

27. Why does Stewie have to disguise himself as a girl called Stephanie when the Griffins are forced to hide out in Texas?

28. When Peter manages to change the past by travelling back to 1984, which 1980s film star does he find himself married to in the present?

29. What happened to Peter when he ate more than 30 hamburgers in one sitting?

30. And how did he cure himself?

31. What is the name of Brian's teenage son, who he never knew he had?

32. Who does Peter discover is working in a used record store in Quahog?

33. When the Griffins decide to buy a younger dog to replace Brian, what do they call him?

34. And what happens to that dog?

35. What happens to Peter after he takes part in numerous medical tests?

36. The episode 'Three Kings' parodies three Stephen King tales. The Shawshank Redemption, Stand By Me and which other story?

37. When Stewie manages to clone himself, what does he call his much dimmer doppelganger?

38. What is the name of the girl with Down Syndrome that Chris briefly dates?

39. What was Quagmire's father's name before she became a male-to-female transsexual?

40. And what name does she go by afterwards?

41. When Brian and Stewie are targeted by bullies in the episode 'Halloween On Spooner Street', what colour do they spray paint the dog?

42. When Peter destroys his kidneys with a home-made energy drink, who ends up donating a kidney to him?

43. After Peter and Chris are locked up in the basement of a Nazi war criminal, who rescues them?

44. In the episode, 'The Big Bang Theory', which famous artist is revealed to be a direct ancestor of Stewie?

45. The characters in Family Guy, American Dad and The Cleveland Show were all hit by the same hurricane. What was it called?

46. What's unusual about the Griffins' houseguest, Billy Finn, in the episode 'Be Careful What You Fish For'?

47. And which British actor voiced that character?

48. When Peter creates his own children's TV show, Petey's Funhouse, what does he call the puppet version of Lois?

49. What was the name of the very first episode of Family Guy?

50. And finally, what was the name of Seth MacFarlane's animated shorts that were eventually developed into Family Guy?

FAMILY GUY™

Season 11
Episode guide

All 23 Episodes

We take a look...

Whenever the Griffins are around you know that things are likely to get unusual. That's certainly true in Season 11 of Family Guy, which offers plenty more Quahog based madness. Actually that's not quite true, as this season doesn't just stick to Rhode Island, as Peter and co. also head to Mount Everest and even go into space, while Brian and Stewie go on holiday to Vegas and the whole family move to the countryside! That's not all, as Mayor West gets accused of murder, Quagmire accidentally gets married, Herbert's dreams come true when Chris moves in with him, and we discover the truth about how Joe was paralysed.

We take a look through all 23 episodes, giving you an intro to the plot, as well as other info about this latest season of Griffin madness.

EPISODE 1

INTO FAT AIR

CAN THE GRIFFINS MAKE IT TO THE TOP OF MOUNT EVEREST?

Peter's not happy when Lois makes him have dinner with Ross Fishman, a man he hates because Lois dated him before they married. Peter's determined that Ross isn't going to make himself out to be better than him, which is difficult as Ross has a good job and likes to go on adventures. When Ross says his family is planning to go to the summit of Mount Everest, Peter can't resist saying that the Griffins are planning to do that too.

After dinner, Peter tells Lois that he knows they can't really go to the top of the mountain, but to his surprise she says, "I think we should do it", as she thinks it will help the family to feel like they can actually achieve something.

Soon the Griffins are off on a plane to the Himalayas, although Stewie's slightly confused about why everyone else thinks this is a good idea, especially as none of them has any mountaineering experience. Even Brian's

happy about it, as he thinks that if he can pee at the top of Mount Everest, all other dogs will know that he owns it (the rule is, the highest pee wins). Once in Nepal, the Griffins get their supplies ready and head off to Everest base camp, where they run into the Fishmans.

Once again Peter can't help but get into a game of one-upmanship with Ross, betting him that the Griffins will beat the Fishmans to the top of the mountain. Ross thinks it's a safe bet, as he doesn't reckon Peter and his family will have the nerve to even try to scale the massive mountain.

Brian has a plan though, as while the Fishmans plan to go up the North Face of Everest, he thinks the Griffins have got a better chance of beating them by going up the South Face.

Can the Griffins beat the Fishmans to the top, and if their competitors get into difficulties, will Peter be able to put their difference aside and help Ross and his family survive the dangerous mountain?

FAMILY GUY FACT:

This isn't the first time we've met Ross Fishman, as in the Season 3 episode 'Stuck Together, Torn Apart', Lois catches up with Ross over coffee. When Peter finds out, he gets jealous and decides he and Lois need to have a trial separation.

RATINGS GUY

PETER FINALLY GETS POWER OVER TELEVISION!

Peter is excited when he gets a letter from Nielsen, the company that measures the size of TV audiences in the US. They want the Griffins to become a Nielsen family, meaning the family's television consumption will be monitored to help create ratings for TV shows. Soon a box has been installed that will let Nielsen know what Peter, Lois and the kids are watching.

It doesn't take long for local news anchor Tom Tucker to turn up on the Griffins' doorstep, as he's heard they've become a Nielsen family. He knows that if he can get the Griffins to tune in, it will help make his ratings look bigger. Tom asks Peter if there's anything he can do to make the news more appealing to him.

Initially Peter just asks Tom to shave off his moustache, but soon realises that he's got some power and starts asking for increasingly extreme things, such as asking Tom to wear a festive hat, and getting him to try to pull-start a very cold chainsaw on air. When Tom does all those things, Peter gets even increasingly power mad, realising that perhaps he can abuse his position to get more of TV to change according to his whims. Peter soon realises with only one ratings box, he only has power over local programming. When the man

from Nielsen returns, Peter runs out to the man's van and steals loads more boxes, so that when he watches a programme, it looks like hundreds of thousands of people have tuned in. Peter decides to phone the production office of Mad Men, but Jon Hamm doesn't think he needs the Quahog resident's tips on making his show less boring. As a result Peter stops watching Mad Men, which causes the show's rating to go through the floor. Because of this, a week later Jon Hamm calls Peter and is more than happy to receive his advice.

Other shows are soon forced to bend to Peter's will, which he thinks is great, even if it means everyone else in the US has to watch whatever stupid things Peter thinks would be good. Other viewers soon get so annoyed that an angry mob descends on the Griffin house, who don't like the idea of having a real cougar on Cougar Town or any of Peter's other terrible ideas.

With his friends turning their backs on him, will Peter learn his lesson and restore TV to the way it was, or does he enjoy being a Nielsen god too much?

FAMILY GUY FACT:

The Nielsen ratings are based on the viewing habits of around 35,000 families, whose TV choices are taken as the average for the 115 million television equipped households in the US.

THE OLD MAN AND THE BIG C

CARTER GETS CANCER... BUT DOESN'T SEEM TOO BOTHERED

Peter, Joe, Brian and Quaqmire head for a baseball match, but the boys are shocked when, in a scramble to catch a ball, Quagmire stands up and his hairpiece has fallen off – Glenn is actually bald! It's not just Peter and co. who get a laugh, as the moment has been caught by the stadium cameras and soon Quagmire's wig falling off has become an internet sensation. The hairless sex hound decides that perhaps the only way to ride out the storm is to embrace his baldness and stop wearing a toupee. That doesn't last long, as it quickly becomes clear that having no hair is turning him into a crotchety old man. Quagmire decides to go the hospital to get a hair transplant, taking Peter, Joe and Brian along with him for moral support. Once there, Brian has more than Quagmire's head to worry about when he accidentally overhears a doctor tell Lois' father, Carter Pewterschmidt, that he has terminal cancer. Brian isn't sure what to do, but shares the news with

Stewie. The baby checks it's true on a CCTV device he's had installed in Carter's house, and when he realises his grandfather really is ill, he can't help but be pleased about how Lois will react. "Oh, this is going to destroy her!" he says. "Oh, just thinking about it makes me all giddy."Deciding that he has to tell Lois, Brian breaks the news to her about her dad's illness. Understandably she's very upset and so she heads to her parents' house to find out how sick Carter is. While initially her mother won't allow her into the house – which Lois finds suspicious – she's even more shocked when she enters and finds Carter in his study, completely healthy.

Lois thinks Brian must have been making it up, but the dog and Stewie know Carter really was ill and so decide to work out what's going on, and why he now seems perfectly fine. Their first thought is that Carter has been replaced by a double so that his illness won't affect the stock price of his company. They set out to prove someone is masquerading as Carter, but soon discover that the truth is even stranger – Mr. Pewterschmidt has a cure for cancer that he's been hiding from the world.

Can the Griffins convince Carter that he needs to release his cure to stop people suffering, or is the rich old man too selfish for that?

FAMILY GUY FACT:

We probably shouldn't be surprised that Quagmire is bald, as in the Season 7 episode, 'FOX-y Lady', we discovered that on his driving license it says he's 61-years-old.

YUG YLIMAF

TIME IS RUNNING BACKWARDS AND ONLY BRIAN AND STEWIE CAN STOP IT

After getting into a competition of 'who's the bigger man' with a guy in a bar over a girl called Cindy, Brian finally wins out by telling her he has a time machine. He takes her back to the Griffins' house and while Stewie is sleeping, he uses the baby's machine to take Cindy back in time to events such as Lincoln being shot and the Hindenburg crashing.

As it works so well, Brian decides to bring other women to see the time machine. Initially it seems like a great idea, but he realises he's got a problem when one of his dates points out that Stewie will know Brian's been using his machine. There's a panel showing the number of years it's travelled. The woman says, "Look, it's no big deal. Just reverse it and take off the miles. That's what I do when I take my dad's car out."

Brian decides to do just that, but as he reverses the dials, the machine flashes and sparks. Stewie wakes up and runs to the machine to work out what's gone wrong with it. Before he can sort it out, a giant beam of light shoots from the top of the machine and Brian and Stewie are blown across the room and knocked unconscious.

When they wake up, Stewie is furious at Brian for messing around with his machine, but soon realises that things are worse than he first realised, as the dog's messing with the dials has reversed the passage of time. Although people still talk normally and don't realise anything is strange, all their actions are going in reverse. Stewie realises quite how drastic this is when Lois gives him a diaper change, puts a filthy nappy on him, and then the contents go back up inside him!

The baby and the dog try to work out how to get time to go forwards again, but nothing seems to work. They see all sorts of strange sights, such as Peter fighting the Giant Chicken in reverse and the fat man falling up the stairs. As time continues to go backwards, events from earlier episodes are seen going backwards. The effects continue to get worse, starting to affect Stewie and Brian too, with the reversion accelerating so that they're moving backwards in time ever faster. Stewie realises that if they don't sort things out quickly, he'll get to his birth and then he'll become unborn!

Can Stewie and Brian sort things out and get time going in the right direction again?

FAMILY GUY FACT:

This is the second time Stewie and Brian's time travelling antics have resulted in them re-experiencing events that happened in the Pilot episode, following the Season 10 episode, 'Back To The Pilot'.

200 EPISODES LATER

FAMILY GUY CELEBRATES ITS BICENTENNIAL

JOE'S REVENGE

THE TRUTH OF HOW JOE BECAME PARALYSED

Who would have believed that 14 years after its January 1999 debut, the upstart animated show Family Guy would be celebrating its 200th episode! That's especially true as in its early days, the show was cancelled twice, before being brought back and becoming a ratings powerhouse.
This special behind-the-scenes features interviews with the cast and crew, such as creator Seth MacFarlane and voice actors Alex Borstein and Seth Green, as well as plenty of classic clips from the show.

Joe is at The Drunken Clam with Peter and Quagmire when the local news announces that wanted fugitive, Bobby "The Shirt" Briggs, has finally been caught after 15 years on the lam. Quagmire isn't sure why Joe is looking so shocked, until the policeman tells him, "Bobby Briggs is the one who put me in this wheelchair."

Joe has always said he was crippled during a Christmas time fight with a Grinch-like creature. However, he admits that he lied because he was ashamed of the real story: that he let a vicious criminal get away. He tells them how he'd gone undercover to take down heroin dealer Briggs, but the criminal realised Joe was wearing a wire. Briggs then repeatedly shot Joe in the legs, crippling him for life.

Joe is elated that Briggs has been caught and decides to hold a party, feeling that he's finally going to get justice. His excitement doesn't last long when the news comes through that Briggs has escaped again!

Realising that Briggs being on the loose is eating Joe up, Peter and Quagmire convince him that he needs to go after the bad guy himself, and they're going to help. Although Joe isn't sure about this as it's a breach of protocol, he eventually agrees. Their investigation leads them to Atlantic City.

Can Peter, Joe and Quagmire catch Bobby Briggs and finally get the policeman some justice?

FAMILY GUY FACT:

As Stewie points out, while 200 episodes is an impressive milestone, it's still less than half of the 500+ episodes of The Simpson that had aired by the time '200 Episode Later' was first shown on US TV.

FAMILY GUY FACT:

Joe first lied to the guys about a Grinch-like character having paralysed him in the episode where we first met him, 'A Hero Sits Next Door'.

EPISODE 7

LOIS COMES OUT OF HER SHELL

LOIS IS FEELING OLD AND STEWIE GETS A TURTLE

It's nearly Lois' birthday, but she doesn't want to make a fuss as she isn't keen on being reminded that she's getting older. As usual, Peter doesn't listen to his wife and decides to organise a surprise birthday party.

Meanwhile, Lois decides to take Stewie to the park. The baby finds a turtle that he calls Sheldon, which he decides to take home. When it's time for Lois' party, Stewie discovers that one of Rupert's eyes has been pulled out. After the baby has left, the turtle spits out Rupert's eye.

The party makes Lois feel worse, especially when Peter gives a speech, saying "Lois, you may not be the young filly you were when I met you, but you're still my reliable old plough horse who's there each day to pull the plough, to help around the barn, and let the husband horse-slap a batch at her now and then. Well, I guess that's it. I love you, sweetheart."

The next day Lois is acting strangely, buying a Jeep, getting highlights in her hair and saying she wants to go to the beach to play Ultimate Frisbee. Brian immediately realises that Lois is having a midlife crisis, something that's soon proved correct when Lois gets younger friends and starts talking about 'sick new tats', as well as dressing like a 20-year-old. Peter starts to get into Lois' new life, such as having spontaneous sex on the washing machine and taking pills in a nightclub.

More strange things start happening to Stewie, such as cutting himself on a razor blade that's been put in place of a bookmark, and narrowly escaping having a cabinet fall on him. He starts to suspect Sheldon is behind it when he finds the turtle standing over him when he wakes up. The animal pulls a knife and Stewie realises the turtle is evil, so he grabs it and flushes it down the toilet.

Soon Lois' constant partying and desperation for youth begins to exhaust Peter, who just wants his wife back. Then, when she sneaks into a Justin Bieber concert hoping to seduce the young star, Peter decides Lois has gone too far.

Can Peter find a way to win his wife back and make her feel better about herself? And will Stewie survive when Sheldon returns wanting revenge?

FAMILY GUY FACT:
Lois also had a bit of a midlife crisis in the Season 8 episode 'Go, Stewie, Go!', which resulted in her making out with Meg's friend.

FRIENDS WITHOUT BENEFITS

MEG GETS A CRUSH ON A GAY GUY

The ever unlucky in love Meg has a massive crush on a new guy at school, Kent, but feels he's too popular to be interested in her. She's obsessed though, having filled her diary with thoughts about him, as well as daydreaming about having sex with him in space. After talking it over with Lois, Meg decides to pluck up the courage to speak to Kent.

When she introduces herself, Kent doesn't know who she is, even though they share English, math and bio classes, as well as the Facebook campaign to get Meg to kill herself. He agrees to hang out with her though, which she takes to mean they're going on a date. They go to the movies and when it gets to the end of the night, Meg leans in for a kiss, but Kent pushes her away, telling her, "I didn't think this was a date."

He explains, "I'm sorry, Meg. I think you're great, and I love hanging out with you, but there's something you should know. I'm gay." He then drops another bombshell, telling Meg that he actually fancies Chris.

Meg is distraught, but Brian tells her, "Maybe he thought he was straight, but then realized he's gay. He's probably still figuring things out. Hang in there." Meg decides that he's still figuring things out, she's going to get him to figure out he's straight!

At school Meg tells Kent he can't be gay, because he likes football, wears cheap clothing and only uses "hello" as a greeting, not as a way to outdo an imaginary antagonist in conversation. However, her plan backfires when Kent tells her he doesn't think he can be her friend if she keeps trying to change him.

She decides that even if he'll never be with her, she can't live without knowing what it's like to sleep with Kent, deciding that, "I mean, if I can't have Kent, then that's the next best thing. I've just got to get Chris to sleep with him."

Unsurprisingly Chris isn't very keen on this, but Meg is determined and cooks up a plan. She tells Kent her brother wants to go on a date him, then drugs Chris in the hope Kent will have sex with him while he's knocked out!

Will Kent and Chris end up sleeping together, and will Meg learn her lesson?

FAMILY GUY FACT:

This episode is called 'Friends Without Benefits', but Mila Kunis, who voices Meg, starred in the movie 'Friends With Benefits' alongside Justin Timberlake.

EPISODE 9

JESUS, MARY AND JOSEPH

FAMILY GUY DOES THE NATIVITY

It's Christmas in Quahog and the Griffins are decorating their tree. Peter decides to tell his family the story of the Nativity. We then travel back 2,000 years, where Peter is Joseph, who's busy doing his carpentry when a women called Mary (who is Lois) turns up. Joseph decides to ask her on a date. After they've been seeing each other for a while, Joseph is getting frustrated that Mary won't put out (she's even got a virginity coach in the form of Hispanic maid, Consuela).

Joseph decides he's going to ask Mary to marry him, but before he gets the chance, she announces that's she's pregnant. Joseph is confused about how that could happen from only his finger, but she explains that God has blessed her with a child. Joseph decides that if it's God's will it's fine.

Several months later, Mary and Joseph are riding a donkey (who is Meg) to Bethlehem – so that they can watch Cher in concert. At the same time Joe, Cleveland and Quagmire as the three wise men are travelling across the desert, heading for Bethlehem too. They stop off at King Herod's Palace, and when they meet the King – who looks an awful lot like Carter Pewterschmidt – they let slip that they're looking for a baby who will be the King Of Kings. Herod isn't impressed by this and vows to kill the child.

In Bethlehem, Mary and Joseph are looking for a room, but the inn owner (Mort) doesn't want to help them. When Joseph explains Mary's about to give birth, he agrees they can use the stable out back. The Three Wise Men turn up looking for the Son Of God, bearing gifts of frankincense, myrrh and a breast pump.

Mary's contractions are getting closer and soon she's given birth to Jesus – who you won't be surprised he to hear is Stewie. The Wise Men aren't the only visitors, as a little drummer boy (Chris) also shows up. He says he has no gift, so Peter decides they'll take his drum.

Not long afterwards Herod shows up, wanting to kill the baby!

Will Jesus survive, and will the Holy Family have to escape to Egypt as they do in the Bible, or is there a more Family Guy way out of the predicament?

FAMILY GUY FACT:

As Stewie points out, Brian is an atheist and refuses to believe in Jesus, even though he personally met the Son Of God in the episode 'I Dream Of Jesus'.

SPACE CADET

FAMILY GUY HEADS INTO ORBIT

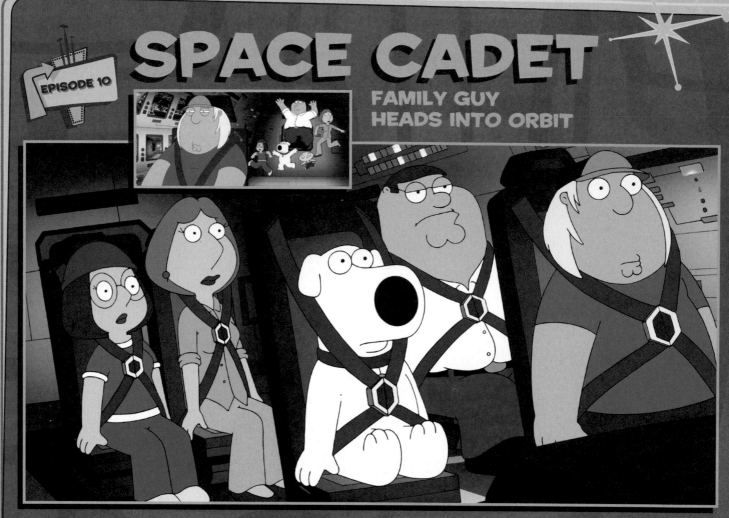

Peter and Lois are called in to James Woods High School to talk about Chris, who's been having a few problems in his lessons and keeps getting into trouble. Later that evening Lois talks to Peter about Chris and what they should do about him. Peter's not hopeful, saying "Let's face it, Lois, the kid's an idiot. What the hell happened to all the smart genes in this family? I mean, I invent the razor blade comb, and my kids are doing nothing!" Lois isn't much more hopeful, adding, "I mean, when Chris grows up, will he even be able to get a job or take care of himself? And what's he going to do when we die?"

They're shocked when Chris emerges and demands that they stop making fun of him, especially as he was only sneaking around in the hope of hearing them having sex. Although Lois and Peter try to convince their son they don't think he's stupid, he doesn't believe them. They then decide perhaps they ought to send Chris off to a camp to build his self-esteem and hopefully help him in school.

Chris decides he likes the idea when he sees Space Camp, where you can learn from real astronauts. Lois tries to dissuade him, feeling it's too advanced for her rather dim son, but he's determined and so they agree to let him go.

Once he's in Florida, Chris gets to see a space-ready Shuttle (kept in case of emergencies), but soon realises he might be out of his depth when he discovers there are going to be things like lectures on orbital dynamics. He ends up phoning home, telling Lois that he hates it at camp and wants to come back to Quahog. They agree to come and pick him up.

When the Griffins get to Florida, Chris tells them the only thing he liked was the Shuttle and decides he'll take his family on a tour of it. While telling his folks about the craft, he mentions that the big red button is the one you press to launch. Stewie impulsively runs over and pushes it, which fires the rockets and initiates the launch sequence. Soon they're off the Launchpad and the Griffins have been lifted into orbit. While they wait for Mission Control to work out how to get them back, Peter decides to go for a spacewalk. Things get more problematic when communications go down and they lose touch with Earth.

Has Chris learned enough in Space Camp to get the Griffins out of orbit?

FAMILY GUY FACT:

Peter's previously been in space in the episodes 'Baby Not On Board' and 'Internal Affairs'.

EPISODE 11

BRIAN'S PLAY

BRIAN BECOMES A LITERARY SUCCESS, BUT STEWIE'S OUT TO UPSTAGE HIM

Few people bought Brian's novel, 'Faster Than The Speed Of Love', but his literary ambition continued as it's the opening night of his new play, 'A Passing Fancy', at the Quahog Playhouse. Everyone seems to like his show about a mismatched couple whose relationship starts to fall apart after the man promises they'll be able to start a family once his acting career takes off, but who keeps putting it off as he chases ever more success. The reviews are great and Brian is on top of the world.

Stewie decides that if Brian can write a play, so can he. Brian thinks this is a joke and that what Stewie has come up with will be rubbish, but when he finally gets round to looking at Stewie's work, 'An American Marriage', he realises that it's a masterpiece. He decides to chat with his cousin Jasper about it, telling him, "I've never read anything like it in my life. It was insightful and fresh and intelligent. It's like his play is mocking me. He wrote it in a night." Jasper advises Brian to tell Stewie his play is rubbish.

When Brian discovers Stewie only has one copy of the play, he sneaks into the baby's room at night and steals it. In the morning Stewie asks Brian if he knows what's happened to his manuscript. Brian tries to change the subject, but then Stewie reveals that actually he found his script buried in the backyard next to one of Brian's bones. Stewie rails at the dog, "You tried to destroy it, didn't you? I knew my play was good. Just like I knew your play was a mediocre patchwork of hackneyed ideas and tired clichés. You have no idea how hard it was to sit in that theatre with all those braying hyenas. Couldn't you tell something was up when Chris and the fat man could follow the plot?" Not long afterwards Stewie finds Brian backstage at the Quahog Playhouse and announces that 'An American Marriage' is going to be produced on Broadway. He's even taking one of Brian's actors with him. Even so, when Brian hears all the best playwrights will be at the opening of Stewie's play, he agrees to go, but is mortified when the likes of David Mamet, Allan Bennett and Yasmina Reza say they've seen 'A Passing Fancy' and they think it absolutely stinks.

Can Stewie do anything to help the distraught Brian and let him feel like he's had at least some measure of success?

FAMILY GUY FACT:
Part of the plot of this episode parodies the play and movie Amadeus, signified by Mozart's 29th Symphony playing as Brian reads Stewie's play.

THE GIGGITY WIFE

QUAGMIRE GETS MARRIED AGAIN...THIS TIME TO A HOOKER

P eter, Glenn and Joe head off for a wild night out, which starts at Harvard University and continues at a strip club, before getting increasingly out of hand as they drunkenly visit an aquarium, steal a shark, and sail a ship down a city street. The boys wake the next morning on the Griffins' front lawn. Quagmire can't remember what happened the night before and gets a major shock when a woman called Charmese emerges and announces that she and Glenn got married. She also reveals her profession when she says, "By the way, I need you to call my pimp and tell him I quit."

Quagmire can't believe he married a prostitute. He tells Charmese they've got to fix this mistake straight away, but she says, "Like hell we do, sweet cream. This is just what I've always wanted: to settle down, find a

husband and live the married life." She's convinced that after 40 years as a hooker, she knows true love and this is it. Glenn doesn't think so and decides he's got to go to the courthouse and get a divorce. Joe warns him to be careful as Quahog has draconian divorce laws that favour the woman. The only way around it is to get the woman to consen to the separation, which isn't going to be easy considering how happy Charmese is.

Perhaps the only way is to try and make the marriage work, so Quagmire decides to give it a go. Glenn puts some effort into his new union, but there's one thing he's really not sure about. It's the one thing he'll normally do with anyone – sex. Charmese gets angry that he won't sleep her and says she hopes she didn't marry a gay guy.

Glenn suddenly sees a possible way out – tell his wife he only likes men. After she catches him watching straight porn, Charmese calls Quagmire on his charade, and says that she'll only consent to the divorce if he proves he really is gay by sleeping with a man while she watches. With no other way out, Glenn heads over to Peter's house to ask if he'll be the ultimate friend.

Will Peter and Glenn really have sex to get rid of Charmese?

FAMILY GUY FACT:

This is Glenn's second marriage that lasted less than one episode. He was briefly married to Joan in 'I Take Thee Quagmire'.

CHRIS CROSS

THE ELDEST GRIFFIN SON TRIES LIVING WITH HERBERT

EPISODE GUIDE

Chris is feeling bad after he's teased about having no-brand sneakers. When he gets home, he asks for better shoes, but Peter tells him, "Shut up and stop complaining. When I was your age, I didn't even have sneakers. We wore stale hamburger buns." Fed up with his parents' attitude, he decides to steal the money he needs, taking several $20 notes from Lois' purse. What he doesn't know is that Meg is watching.

On the way back from a birthday party, Stewie's bad mood is turned around when he hears the singing of Canadian songstress Anne Murray. He says, "She sounds like an angel. It's like her voice is putting my entire body in her mouth." Stewie soon becomes obsessed with the singer, getting lost in fantasies whenever he hears her sing. However, when Brian finds out, he rubbishes Murray, saying he thinks she's awful.

Meg tells Chris that she saw him steal the money, but promises not to tell if he does whatever she tells him to do. He agrees and she gives him a list of stuff to get done. After doing things such as cleaning her room and completing her homework, he starts to get annoyed with her increasingly extreme demands. He decides that he doesn't want to do Meg's chores and doesn't want to be grounded to for stealing, so he runs away.

Chris heads down the road to Herbert's house and asks to live with him. The elderly man, who's always been a little too interested in young men, is delighted, saying "My goodness, I feel like I wanna pinch myself to see if I'm dreamin'."

At first the living arrangements seem to work quite well, with Herbert trying to groom Chris, but the young Griffin too dim to see what's happening. However, when Chris starts messing with things in Herbert's house, the old man decides perhaps having a young man staying isn't the dream he imagined.

Stewie has managed to convince Brian that Anne Murray is great, but the baby starts to get annoyed at Brian's interpretation of her song 'Snowbird'. As they're now fans, they decide to go and visit the famed singer to ask her whether the tune is about a relationship or the fear of growing old. Stewie's less impressed though when he discovers she didn't actually write the song herself.

Will Chris stay with Herbert or will he end up back home, and will his parents even realise he's missing?

FAMILY GUY FACT:

This episode suggests Stewie had a twin brother called Dave, who didn't survive – probably because of Stewie as he was born in a coffin.

VALENTINE'S DAY IN QUAHOG

LOVE COMES TO QUAHOG, BUT THAT MAY NOT BE A GOOD THING

CALL GIRL

LOIS BECOMES A PHONE SEX OPERATOR

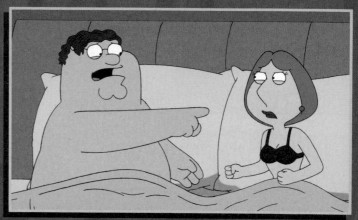

Romance is in the air, with a series of stories featuring the Valentine's plans of Quahog's residents. Peter and Lois decide to spend the whole of Valentine's Day in bed, Meg heads off on a date with a guy she met on the Internet, which turns bad when he knocks her out and steals her kidney – although she doesn't think that's a complete deal-breaker.

Quagmire gets cursed by a one-night stand, which results in everyone seeing him as a woman; including Joe, who hits on him; and Dr. Hartman, who wants to give him a pelvic exam. Consuela heads back to Mexico to see her husband. Herbert's grand-niece falls for Chris and turns to her uncle for romantic advice. Stewie has oedipal problems when a time-travel trip to the 60s sees him chatting up a baby Lois.

Brian gets depressed about his lack of success in love, so Stewie rounds up all the dog's former girlfriends to tell him where he went wrong. And finally Mayor West discovers his wife Carol has been seeing another mayor behind his back! Will love win the day in all these Valentine's tales?

Peter decides to buy a falcon. He gets so excited about his new purchase that he steals a motorbike and sidecar so that he can take the bird for a ride. Unfortunately the man who owns the vehicle isn't impressed and so sues Peter for all he's worth. With their finances ruined, Lois realises she's going to have to go back to work. She gets approached by a man who tells her he can get her voice work. Lois thinks this means she'll be doing voiceovers for commercials, but it turns out they actually want her to work on a phone sex line. While Lois initially doesn't want to do it, she changes her mind when she learns she can earn $2,000 a week.

Lois adopts the phone sex name Classy and starts fulfilling the vicarious sexual pleasures of the likes of Joe, Quagmire and Mort. However, talking about sex all day means she isn't that interested in sleeping with Peter. He gets annoyed about this and so Joe suggests he phones Classy. When he does so, he doesn't realise he's talking to Lois, but she knows it's her hubby who's called up. Very quickly Peter falls for the voice on the end of the phone and wants to meet, perhaps to have sex in real life! *Will Peter go through with meeting Classy, and can Lois forgive him for falling for another woman (even though technically it's her)?*

FAMILY GUY FACT:

We discover the full names of two Family Guy regulars in this episode. Wooden sea-dog Seamus' surname is Levine, while Herbert's first name is John.

FAMILY GUY FACT:

Giovanni Ribisi voices Randy, the man who hires Lois to work on the phone sex lines. He also worked with Seth MacFarlane on the Family Guy creator's film, Ted.

EPISODE 16

TURBAN COWBOY

PETER ACCIDENTALLY BECOMES A TERRORIST!

Peter, Joe and Quagmire are fed up with how boring their lives have become and so they decide to try something new – skydiving. Peter falls in love with the sport, using it to fall into places such as his house for dinner and the library when he needs to return a book. However, when he decides to phone Lois during a fall, he forgets to open his chute and ends up impaling himself on the replica of the Eiffel Tower at the Paris hotel in Las Vegas.

He ends up in the hospital where he meets Mahmoud. Peter's initially scared of the man because he's wearing a skullcap, but Mahmoud explains that he's a Muslim and it's just a prayer hat. Peter is intrigued and wants to learn more about his friend's culture. While Joe and Quagmire aren't sure about Peter's new friend, he's smitten, especially when he discovers that in Muslim cultures, woman tend to be subservient to the men.

Soon Peter and Mahmoud are going together to a Muslim bar called The Chaste Camel, and Peter is buying strange things such as cobras at the market (which he's decided is actually a bazaar). Mahmoud is impressed with how stereotypically Muslim his new friend is becoming and so invites him to a secret meeting with some other followers of Islam.

The other men aren't sure Peter should be there, but are soon convinced he's Muslim enough. They then reveal the reason they're there – to plan how to blow up the Quahog bridge. However, Peter thinks they're just playing.

When he tells Joe about what's been going on, the policeman convinces Peter that he's joined a terrorist sleeper cell, and that they may be able to prevent the bombing if Peter goes undercover wearing a wire. When the terrorists realise Peter's working as a double agent, they decide they must blow up the bridge immediately.

Can Peter stop the bombing, or is he so dim he's actually going to cause it?

FAMILY GUY FACT:
Although Meg is seen several times in this episode, she doesn't get a single line of dialogue.

EPISODE 17
12 AND A HALF ANGRY MEN

EPISODE 18
BIGFAT

HAS MAYOR WEST COMMITTED MURDER?

THE WILDERNESS IS NO PLACE FOR A RHODE ISLANDER

Joe, Quagmire and Peter are enjoying a drink at the Drunken Clam when news comes over the police radio that there's a possible homicide at the Mayor's house. Later that evening the news reports that an aide to Mayor West has been found murdered and the police have found a blackmail note saying the victim was going to reveal the Mayor's corruption. As the aide was killed by a knife belonging to Mayor West, he's the number one suspect, and so gets arrested.

Some time later Mayor West is on trial for murder, and Peter, Bruce, Tom Tucker, Seamus, Consuela, Brian, Quagmire, Doctor Hartman, Carl, Mort, Carter, and Herbert have been chosen as the jury. After the closing arguments, the jury goes off to the deliberation room, where most of them seem to think it's a foregone conclusion – all the evidence points to him and so Mayor West is guilty.

When jury foreman Bruce calls for a vote, eleven people immediately vote guilty, but Brian holds out, saying he doesn't think there's enough evidence to convict the Mayor 'beyond reasonable doubt'. Everyone else thinks he's just deliberately being awkward, but Brian slowly lays out his thoughts, such as the fact the blackmail note was written on hotel stationery and that the person who supposedly witnessed the murder was 100 yards away and engaged in an orgy! Can *Brian* convince the others that Mayor West is innocent?

Stewie's getting a little fat, so Peter, Joe and Quagmire are building a jungle gym for him in the Griffins' backyard. While they're working, Glenn tells them that the best strip clubs in the world are in Montreal.

Joe and Peter decide that Quagmire needs to take them to Canada so they can see the strippers for themselves. Glenn agrees and organises a private jet (which he got because he saw John Travolta cheating on his wife) to take them north. On the flight, Peter decides to play a trick, where he goes out on the wing of the plane. His antics don't prove to be very funny when he sends the aircraft into a spin and it crashes.

The boys are now lost in the Canadian wilderness, which gets even worse when Quagmire breaks his legs. After a couple of days they decide their only hope is to send Peter off to see if he can find civilisation. Not long after he's left, a Canadian man saves Joe and Glenn and tells them that Peter has gone off in a direction where there's nothing but wilderness for thousands of kilometres. Two months later Peter is still lost and despite Lois' protestations, the authorities are about to give up the search. However, they eventually find Peter, who after so long in the wild has gone feral and forgotten how to speak!

Will Peter ever be able to reintegrate himself back into modern civilisation?

FAMILY GUY FACT:
The title and plot of this episode are a loose parody of Reginald Rose's Twelve Angry Men, which was originally a 1954 TV play before becoming an Oscar nominated movie in 1957.

FAMILY GUY FACT:
Peter going out on the wing of the plane is a reference to a famous episode of The Twilight Zone, where William Shatner sees a creature on an airplane's wing, but no one believes him.

TOTAL RECALL

LOIS MAKES FRIENDS WITH JOE & QUAGMIRE, AND PETER'S NOT HAPPY ABOUT IT

After a night out bowling, Peter wakes up the next morning feeling a bit ill. When Lois hears his deep, gravelly voice, she finds it incredibly sexy and they end up spending much of the day having sex. Once he's better, Lois isn't as interested in Peter sexually anymore, so he becomes determined to make himself ill again. His plan backfires though when he fails to get a sexy, deep voice, but does make himself so ill that he has to go to the hospital.

As he's sick, Peter can't play in a bowling tournament with Glenn and Joe, so Lois agrees to go in his place. Quagmire doesn't think Lois is going to be any good, but she ends up bowling the winning ball. The three of them end up having drinks at Drunken Clam and the boys realise that Lois is a good friend to have.

Stewie meanwhile is mortified when he searches his room and can't find his teddy Rupert. Brian tells him it's because it was discovered the toy was dangerous and so Lois sent it back to the factory. He gets sent a stuffed giraffe as a replacement, but it's just not the same, so Stewie convinces Brian to drive him to the toy factory so they can save Rupert.

Lois spends the week hanging out with Joe and Quagmire, having a great time. When Peter feels better he finds his wife and friends in the Drunken Clam together. He's a bit upset when he discovers they're about to head off to a baseball game and they don't have a ticket for him. When Lois returns, Peter gets angry with her, telling her that Joe and Glenn are his friends, not her's. She's not impressed about her husband telling her she's only allowed to do groceries and women's things.

Brian and Stewie get to the toy factory and decide to go on a tour, with Stewie saying that at some point they'll sneak off to find Rupert. They work out where the Recall Department is and leave the tour. However, when they get inside, they discover that thousands of identical teddies have been sent back, and Rupert must be somewhere amongst them!

Will Peter and Lois be able to come to come sort of agreement over her new friendships? And can Stewie get his beloved Rupert back?

FAMILY GUY FACT:
In this episode Brian reveals he's had two drink driving convictions in the last six months, and now has to have a breathalyser in his car to start it.

SAVE THE CLAM

HORACE IS KILLED AND IT MAY BE THE END OF THE CLAM!

It's the day of a softball game between the Drunken Clam and Goldman's Pharmacy. Peter, Joe and Quagmire are playing for the Clam and think they're definitely going to win – until they see that Mort has brought in a ringer, their old friend Jerome. Near the end of the game the Clam is ahead. They'll win as long as Jerome doesn't score with the final throw. The ball comes off Jerome's bat like a rocket and barrels straight into Clam owner Horace's forehead, killing him instantly!

Nobody can believe Horace is dead, particularly Quagmire, who at the funeral home starts bawling that it isn't natural to outlive your bartender. The funeral turns out better for Meg though, who ends up giving the mortician a hand dressing a body and is offered a job helping prepare the deceased for burial, which she happily accepts.

After the funeral the boys head to the Clam for a consolatory drink, but find that with the heavily-in-debt Horace dead, the bank has taken possession and closed it. They can't believe that the place that's the cornerstone of their friendship is shut. Peter's particularly worried as he knows that when they do things together that doesn't involve drinking, it normally goes badly. They try out other places to booze, but nowhere's like the Clam.

Meg is doing well at her new job, learning the tricks of the funeral trade. She gets annoyed when Chris turns up and starts messing with the bodies. Then, when she realises a body has gone missing, she knows that her brother must have taken it. She's also determined that if he doesn't bring it back, he'll be the one in the coffin – alive or dead.

Peter decides they ought to break into the Drunken Clam to have a drink despite it being closed, which leads to a night filled with copious amounts of alcohol. In the morning the boys realise that nowhere can replace their beloved drinking hole. With bulldozers outside wanting to knock it to the ground, they decide to lock themselves in and try to save the bar.

Is this the end of The Drunken Clam, and indeed is it the end of Chris?

FAMILY GUY FACT:

'Save The Clam' marks the first time we've met Mort Goldman's parents, who aren't impressed he has no sports awards.

FARMER GUY

PETER GETS INTO AGRICULTURE... AND DRUGS!

Lois doesn't believe it when a news report says that Quahog is in the middle of a crime wave. However, it appears the town really does have a problem, with Quagmire getting mugged, performing seals stealing fish and babies coming out the womb shooting guns. It really hits home when the Griffins get burgled. Lois finally has to agree that Quahog doesn't feel safe anymore.

The impulsive Peter decides to do something about this, so he heads into the countryside where he finds a farm for sale that he thinks will be a wholesome place to raise his family. Chris, Meg, Stewie and Lois aren't sure about this drastic move, but Peter manages to convince them that it'll be good for everyone. Brian isn't so certain, especially when they tell him they're taking him to "a nice, big farm upstate", which is what some parents tell kids when their dog is dead.

Peter starts to get into farm life, such as slowly getting cows to cross a road, forcing his kids to plough a field and having a friend called Larry who he never speaks to. He may be enjoying himself, but when Lois runs the numbers she realises that Peter's failed to grow a single crop and with no income they're in danger of losing the farm. Brian doesn't want to give up and so vows to go to agricultural college to learn the techniques they'll need to make the farm a success.

Not long after Brian has gone, a tornado strikes and so the Griffins head into the storm cellar. They're all a bit surprised to find it full of beakers, test tubes and cold medicine – it's a crystal meth lab!

Lois is horrified and says they'll have to call the police. Peter stops her, saying, "I know you're freaked out, but when you really stop and think about it, this meth lab is our family's best chance to make meth in a lab." He thinks it could be the only way to save the farm. Lois isn't sure, but eventually agrees they can make a bit of meth, just to cover the bills.

This is the Griffins though, so soon things get out of hand and they're running a meth den, producing so much of the drug that a lot of it is ending up back in Quahog and making the crime there even worse.

Are the Griffins going to be drug dealers from now on, or will they realise they're doing a bad thing?

FAMILY GUY FACT:

This isn't the first time Peter has sold their Spooner Street house without telling Lois, as he did the same thing in the Season 2 episode 'Peter, Peter, Caviar Eater'.

NO COUNTRY CLUB FOR OLD MEN

THE GRIFFINS JOIN THE BLUE BLOOD SET

Stewie is delighted when he finds his harmonica wedged in the sofa, but soon he's lost it again. The instrument turns up when Stewie walks into the bathroom and sees his father standing in the bath, holding his bum – Peter's managed to sit on the harmonica and it's slipped up his butt! The doctors tell Peter the surgery to remove the harmonica will be expensive, but when he farts and manages to make a tune, the fat Quahogian decides he doesn't want it taken out anyway. Peter's skill as a butt harmonica player gets him picked to appear on America's Got Talent in LA. Peter's performance wows the audience and the judges, but it all comes crashing down when the harmonica falls out of his bum at the end of his song. The Griffins get to fly back to Rhode Island in First Class, where Chris meets a young woman called Amanda, who seems to like him and invites him and his family to the Barrington Country Club. Brian realises Chris is dating a Barrington, the richest and most exclusive family in Rhode Island.

When they get to the club, it's no surprise that Lois' incredibly rich father, Carter, is also a member. As usual Carter starts to insult Peter, although he's shocked when his son-in-law says they're there to have lunch with the Barringtons. Carter has been trying to get into the Barringtons' inner circle, and now the son-in-law he hates is eating with them. As the Griffins settle down to lunch, Carter keeps muscling in, trying to get Mr. Barrington to notice him. The owner of the country club seems to like Peter but gets increasingly frustrated with Carter. Eventually his patience breaks and he throws Mr. Pewterschmidt out of the club, before offering his membership to Peter. Suddenly the Griffins are part of the country club set, with Carter having to accept the role reversal of being the loser on the outside. Lois thinks this might be a good opportunity for her dad to learn a lesson, and that being the outcast might make him realise how horrible he's been to Peter. Carter's not interested in learning anything and just wants back into the club. Eventually Peter agrees to help and they concoct an outlandish plan to get Barrington to realise Carter is the right material for membership.

Can Carter get back into the club, or will he and Peter both end up kicked to the kerb?

FAMILY GUY FACT:
The Barrington Country club has previously appeared in the episode 'Death Lives', when Peter plays golf there on his wedding anniversary.

EPISODE 24

ROAD TO VEGAS

TWO STEWIES AND TWO BRIANS HEAD TO VEGAS

The Griffins head off to watch Quahog's gay pride parade, which Lois thinks will be educational, even though she laughs when she sees two men who 'think' they're a child's parents. It turns out to be a good day for Brian, who wins two tickets to Las Vegas to see Celine Dion.

After his girlfriend says she doesn't want to go (because Stewie has replaced her with one of his robots), Brian invites the baby to come with him to Vegas. Stewie agrees and says that rather than flying, they should use the teleportation machine he's just completed. However, when he presses the button, nothing seems to happen and Brian and Stewie are still in Quahog.

Meanwhile, in Las Vegas, Stewie and Brian suddenly appear out of nowhere. Miraculously they're now both in Vegas and Quahog, as the teleportation machine has duplicated them, but neither version knows that.

The Stewie and Brian who've arrived in Vegas start to have a great time, watching the Bellagio fountains, winning a huge jackpot on the slot machines and checking into their luxurious hotel room. The other dog and baby aren't doing so well, as when they get to Nevada on the plane, they lose on the slots and find someone's already checked into their room, forcing them

to go to a cheap, horrible hotel. Things get worse for them when they lose all their money gambling and can't even get into the Celine Dion show.

The reason they can't get in is, of course, because the other Stewie and Brian have already taken their seats. The duo are still having an amazing time though, enjoying all that Vegas has to offer.

The Brian and Stewie who didn't get into the show see their luck go from bad to worse, as they've lost all their money and Stewie's even gambled away their plane tickets. After they get a hot tip on a basketball game, they think their only option is to borrow some money from a loan shark and bet it on the match. When the team lose, they know the shady loan shark will kill them if he or his goons find them! However, with two sets of Brian and Stewie in town, the loan shark finds the wrong ones first.

Will both Brians and Stewies manage to get out of Vegas alive?

FAMILY GUY FACT:

This is Family Guy's third trip to Vegas, after Peter & Chris go there in 'When You Wish Upon A Weinstein', and Peter skydives there in 'Turban Cowboy'.

FAMILY GUY

CROSSWORD

Work out the clues and fill in the Family Guy grid.

ACROSS

2. Name of the Griffins' doctor (5,7)
3. Newsman with a son called Jake (3,6)
5. First name of Lois' much-married sister (5)
6. Lois' maiden name (13)
8. Actress who voices Lois (4,8)
9. Family guy patriarch (5,7)
10. Channel 5's monosyllabic weatherman (5,8)
11. Middle name of Stewie (8)
14. First name of Lois' mother (7)
19. Type of sea creature legend says co-founded the town Family Guy is set in (4)
20. Maid who often wants more furniture polish (8)
23. African-American former neighbour of the Griffins (9,5)
27. First name of Brian's gay cousin (6)
28. Eldest daughter of Peter and Lois (3,7)
30. Elderly Griffin neighbour who's a little too interested in young boys (7)
31. Stewie's beloved teddy bear (6)
33. Reality show the Griffins briefly took part in (3,4,4,8)
38. The Griffins' sex-hound neighbour (5,8)
39. First name of the man Peter grew up believing was his dad (7)
40. Murderous former Channel 5 Action News anchor (5,7)
41. Stewie's accidentally born half-brother (7)
42. Actor who voices Chris (4,5)
43. Town in which the show is set (6)

DOWN

1. Brian's home state (5)
4. State in which Family Guy is set (5,6)
7. Surname of Peter's biological father (10)
12. Party Of Five actress who voiced Meg before Mila Kunis took over (5,7)
13. Brian's ex-girlfriend voiced by Drew Barrymore (7)
15. Type of animal that used to live in Chris' closet (6)
16. Job Peter had when he met Lois (5,3)
17. Road on which the Griffins live (7,6)
18. Name of the country briefly run by Peter from his house (7)
21. Creator of Family Guy (4,10)
22. The only blond member of the Griffin Clan (5,7)
24. Peter's middle name (9)
25. Baby daughter of Joe (5)
26. Actor after whom Meg & Chris' high school is named (5,5)
29. Birth country of Peter (6)
32. Onetime Griffin houseguest after he hurt his ankle (5)
33. Surname of Action 5 News' Asian Correspondent (8)
34. Policeman Joe's surname (7)
35. Type of animal Peter often gets in a fight with (7)
36. Word often used by Quagmire when he thinks something is sexual (7)
37. First name of Family Guy's peg-legged and peg-armed sailor (6)

LOIS & PETER GRIFFIN'S
PARENTING TIPS

Would Chris be dim, Meg so needy and Stewie a sexually ambiguous genius without the guidance of Lois and Peter? It's difficult to tell, but Peter and Lois certainly have an unusual parenting style. Here's how to bring up your kids if you want to be like the Griffins.

HOW TO RAISE AN OUTSIDER DAUGHTER

If you want your kid never to fit in and to constantly seek love and approval in all the wrong places, Peter and Lois have got is sewn up. Perhaps the most important thing to do is constantly put the child down. "Shut up, Meg" is pretty much Peter's catchphrase, while telling his daughter she's ugly, not wanted and barely part of the family is par for the course. Peter once shot her as he cares for her so little, and even sold her to pay off his pharmacy tab.

Lois helps too, laughing at the idea of her daughter having a boyfriend, as well as reading her child's diary to the family while laughing. All this ensures that Meg is constantly looking for scraps of attention and will agree to anything that makes her feel like she's fitting in, whether it's joining a suicide cult or offering to hold someone's drug toad for them.

You can also try to live your dreams through this child, such as when Lois forced Meg to practice the piano with a ball and chain attached to her leg to stop her escaping, or Peter making her do bird noises in the hope she'll become famous for it.

> "SORRY KIDS, DADDY LOVES YOU BUT DADDY ALSO LOVES TV, AND IN ALL FAIRNESS TV CAME FIRST"
> **PETER GRIFFIN**

There are things to watch out for though, as constantly putting your daughter down can have unwanted repercussions. Meg quite often threatens to kill herself –although nobody believes her and Lois even once gave her some pills, in case her daughter wanted to go through with it. Meg's been seen trying to force herself on some burglars and ended up being charged with sexual assault. She also once ripped out one of her teeth to show Lois the lengths she'd go to for love. Her most extreme rebellion came after she spent time in prison, returning as a hardened criminal who makes her family live in fear and who holds up a pharmacy.

LESSON:
You can certainly destroy your child's self-esteem if you want to, but be prepared for some payback.

HOW TO RAISE A DIM SON

It probably helps with Chris that Peter isn't the brightest bulb in the pack either, as the boy's dad has been judged to be officially retarded. This means that whenever Chris does anything stupid, his dad is normally doing something even more ridiculous. This can have its drawbacks though, as Peter often has a rather extreme reaction if he thinks Chris has outdone him in some way, such as his jealousy when he discovers Chris has a much larger penis than he has.

Lois meanwhile is always supportive of her son, even if it's in a rather patronising way that ensures he knows she doesn't really expect much from him. That doesn't mean Peter and Lois always just accept their son's stupidity, as they sometimes try to do something about it, such as Peter attempting to convert Chris to Judaism under the logic that this will make him smarter.

Chris does have a few problems that Lois and Peter haven't managed to iron out, such as the fact that he seems to be attracted to his own mother. For example, when Lois was home schooling her kids, he passed Meg a note saying that he thinks 'Mrs. Griffin is hot', while in another episode he says he's going to masturbate to pictures of her.

The Griffin parents also seem bad at nurturing his talents, as while he's shown aptitude at things such as art, films and rock music, Lois and Peter rarely support this for long. Indeed the Griffins' main parenting style for Chris seems to be to simply let him get on with it, unless there's something specific that needs their attention.

LESSON:
Raising a dim kid can be pretty easy, as long as you don't want to put much effort into trying to make the most of the talents they do have.

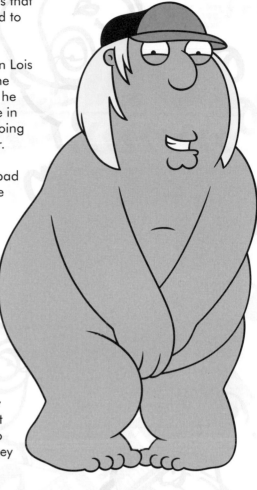

HOW TO RAISE A GENIUS

With Stewie, Lois and Peter's main style of parenting seems to be to have absolutely no clue about the true nature of their baby. When Stewie says something cutting or nasty, they seem to get the gist of what he's saying but not the venom behind it. Indeed they're often negligently ignorant, not noticing that Stewie has built a weapons cache in his room, or that he's invented all manner of incredible devices.

In his early days, Stewie spent much of his time plotting the death of his mother, but she never seemed to notice the endless murder attempts. The only times that she's cottoned on it's either been in a dream or when she was merely a simulation in one of Stewie's inventions.

Luckily for Lois, Stewie has mellowed towards her recently, but his parents' complete ignorance about him remains. In fact there's a case that they are incredibly bad parents, as they don't notice him sneaking out dressed as a woman to go on dates with grown men, or seem to realise when he goes off on a trip with Brian. However, their lack of discipline and attention is probably a good thing, as the one time Lois hit him, it revealed an extreme masochistic streak where Stewie followed her around hoping to be spanked.

It's more than possible Stewie's brains have nothing to do with parenting and everything to do with accident, as in a flashback in the episode 'Stuck Together, Torn Apart', Stewie is shown to be a normal baby with a normal head. However, while jumping on a bed he smacks his noggin, which changes his skull to the shape of an American football and results in him having a new voice and much more adult way of speaking.

LESSON:
Treating a genius baby like a normal one and ignoring what they get up to doesn't seem to stunt their intelligence, but just be aware that they may try to kill you every now and then.

THE TOP 5 MOST
CONTROVERSIAL
⟩⟩⟩⟩⟩⟩⟩⟩⟩⟩ FAMILY GUY EPISODES

FAMILY GUY HAS ALWAYS GONE TO THE EDGE WITH IT'S HUMOUR, AND SOMETIMES IT'S TAKEN THINGS SO FAR THAT IT'S DRAWN A FAIR AMOUNT OF CONTROVERSY. THERE HAS BEEN CRITICISM FROM THE HIGHEST LEVELS AND EVEN ONE INSTALMENT THAT GOT THE ENTIRE SHOW BANNED IN VENEZUELA! HERE ARE THE FIVE MOST CONTROVERSIAL EPISODES:

5. DON'T MAKE FUN OF SARAH PALIN!
EXTRA LARGE MEDIUM
Season 8

WHAT HAPPENS: Chris isn't sure what to do about a girl he fancies, but Stewie convinces him to ask her out, even though the baby is surprised that the object of Chris' affection, Ellen, has Down Syndrome. Chris learns that while he has preconceptions about people with Down Syndrome being special, they can be as difficult as anyone else.

WHY THE CONTROVERSY?: There was criticism over a joke where Ellen says her mother is the former governor of Alaska. This is a reference to the fact that former Vice Presidential candidate and Alaskan governor, Sarah Palin, has a son called Trig who has Down Syndrome. Palin and her daughter, Bristol, publicly criticised the show, with Sarah saying the makers were "cruel, cold-hearted people". However, Andrea Fay Friedman, who has Down Syndrome and voices Ellen, issued a statement criticising Palin for having no sense of humour.

4. NOT ALL SINGING BABIES ARE CUTE
AIRPORT '07
Season 5

WHAT HAPPENS: After Peter causes Quagmire to lose his job, he ends up living with the Griffins, which soon becomes intolerable due to Glenn's sexual fetishes (such as putting his foot in Meg's mouth while she sleeps). To get him out, Peter comes up with a hare-brained scheme to get Quagmire his job back.

WHY THE CONTROVERSY?: Many were shocked by the inclusion in this episode of a cutaway song called 'Prom Night Dumpster Baby', sung by babies who, as the title suggests, were born at a high school prom but then put in a dumpster. The ditty was a reference to the case of Melissa Drexler, who gave birth to a baby at her prom, dumped it in the trash and then returned to the dance. Many thought Family Guy had gone too far by making a song out of infanticide.

3. VENEZUELA HATES MARIJUANA
420
Season 7

WHAT HAPPENS: Brian becomes angry when the police arrest him for carrying a small amount of marijuana. He and Stewie launch a campaign to legalise the drug, winning over the masses with a song that helps get weed decriminalized. However Carter Pewterschmidt bribes Brian to get the drug banned again by promising to publish his novel.

WHY THE CONTROVERSY?: While some felt the episode went to the edge of acceptability by suggesting Marijuana could be a good thing, the real controversy happened in Venezuela, where Hugo Chavez's government was furious at the episode's attitude to drugs (or at least their perception of it) and banned the entire show from airing on any station. They later used a clip of Brian and Stewie's song about marijuana as evidence that the US supports the use of the drug.

2. IS THERE ANYTHING FUNNY ABOUT ABORTION?
PARTIAL TERMS OF ENDEARMENT
Season 8

WHAT HAPPENS: After Lois agrees to be a surrogate mother for an old friend, the biological parents die in a car crash. Lois is left with the decision over whether to have the baby and raise it, or to have an abortion. While she decides on the latter, Peter becomes an anti-abortion activist and tries to stop her (although she has it in the end).

WHY THE CONTROVERSY?: Although the Fox Network in the US allowed the episode to be made, when they saw the final result, they got squeamish and refused to air it due to its abortion theme. The episode ended up making its debut in the UK instead (and was later released in the US on DVD).

The first time scenes from the episode made it to Fox were clips in the '200 Episodes Later' special that aired during the latest season. The controversy grew due to news sources such as Reuters saying it wasn't aired due to a 'graphic depiction of an abortion', which isn't actually in the episode.

1. PETER NEEDS A JEW, BUT SHOULD HE?
WHEN YOU WITH UPON A WEINSTEIN
Season 3

WHAT HAPPENS: Peter wishes that he could find a Jew to help him with his finances. When Max Weinstein turns up after breaking down outside the Griffins' house, Peter takes it as a sign. Peter becomes increasingly convinced that being Jewish is the key to success, and decides to convert Chris to Judaism against Lois' wishes.

WHY THE CONTROVERSY?: This is another episode the Fox Network refused to air, as they were afraid it would be seen as anti-Semitic. That's despite the fact that show creator Seth MacFarlane had shown the script to two rabbis before production to get their approval (they felt it was okay as Peter learns a good lesson by the end). However the Fox executives were right to be worried, as when it finally aired on the Cartoon Network in 2003, the Bourne Company, which owns the song 'When You Wish Upon A Star', sued Family Guy over a little ditty from the episode called 'I Need

A Jew', which parodies their song (but with an altered tune and new lyrics). They objected to what they called the offensive lyrics of the song (which play on perceptions of Jewish stereotypes), but lost their case as parody is protected under US copyright law.

OTHER CONTROVERSIAL EPISODES:

THE CLEVELAND-LORETTA QUAGMIRE Season 4 – In this episode, a cutaway shows Peter as part of a barbershop quartet that breaks bad news to HIV patients by singing them a song called, 'You Have AIDS'. This led to criticism by several prominent AIDS charities.

QUAGMIRE'S DAD *Season 8* – This episode dealt with Quagmire discovering that his father has had a sex change operation. Numerous LGBT organisations felt the episode mocked transgender people, particularly a scene where Brian continuously vomits when he discovers he's slept with someone who was born male.

PETER-ASSMENT *Season 8* There were complaints levelled at this one due to a scene where Stewie takes part in a show called Terry Schiavo: The Musical. Schiavo was a woman in a persistent vegetative state who was at the centre of years of legal wrangling over whether she should be allowed to die.

SCREAMS OF SILENCE: THE STORY OF BRENDA Q *Season 10* – When Quagmire's sister and her boyfriend, Jeff, come to stay, Spooner Street is exposed to Jeff's terrible domestic violence. While the episode sees Jeff get his comeuppance, some thought it was making fun of women being beaten by their partners.

BACK TO THE PILOT *Season 10* – Many in the media thought Family Guy had gone right to the edge with a time-travelling plot that saw Brian & Stewie ensuring that the 9/11 attacks happened, in order to prevent an ever worse nuclear war from occurring later on.

EVIL ANIMALS

Quahog has more than its fair share of animals that turn bad – and as we learn in the latest season, even a turtle can be malevolent. Some animals act nice but turn out to be evil, some hold seemingly endless grudges, while others appears to be bad but are simply misunderstood. Let's meet them...

The Evil Monkey
From: Various episodes starting with 'Dammit Janet!'

Would you believe someone who told you they had an evil monkey in their closet? That was the problem Chris faced, as the chimp would burst from his closet and point at him with an evil look on its face – but nobody would believe it existed.

We first saw the monkey in the Season 2 episode 'Dammit Janet'. After that he became a running joke, popping up numerous times but never when any of the Griffins (except Chris) were around. Chris did get a brief respite in 'The Former Life of Brian' when Brian's son Dylan Flannigan beat the monkey up, allowing Chris to go in his closet for the first time in years – unsurprisingly he discovered it was full of faeces.

Things came to a head in the episode 'Hannah Banana' when Chris managed to capture the monkey and show his family that it was real. Chris then discovered that he'd gotten the animal wrong and that the pointing was just its way of trying to start a conversation. The chimp only moved into Chris' closet because he was in a bad place in his life after he caught his wife cheating on him with another monkey. In the end Chris and the monkey became friends, although the simian decided it was time to move on and ended up staying in the closet of local news anchor Tom Tucker's son, Jake.

Billy Finn
From: 'Be Careful What You Fish For'

Some animals aren't so much evil as incredibly annoying moochers, such as the dolphin Billy Finn. Peter first came across the sea mammal while trying to fish for a Mercedes that had fallen off a cargo ship. After Peter half-heartedly promised Billy a favour in return for a hood ornament from the car, the dolphin decided that meant that Peter had to take him in when he opted to try life on land. Billy soon outstayed his welcome due to his rudeness and annoying sense of humour, but the Griffins couldn't get him out. Eventually Peter realised the only way to get rid of him was to engineer a reunion between Billy and his estranged wife, Joanne.

The Giant Chicken
From: Various episodes starting with 'Da Boom'

It's not just Chris who has an animal nemesis, as Peter's got one too – The Giant Chicken. Their endless grudge began in the episode 'Da Boom', when Peter was given an expired coupon by the chicken, which made the Griffin patriarch so angry that he attacked the oversized avian.

Neither man nor beast were willing to let it lie, and when they met again in 'Blind Ambition', their escalated battle took them to a train station, a cruise ship, and an airport, causing much destruction in the process. In 'No Chris Left Behind' it seemed a truce was on the cards, as Peter and the Chicken couldn't remember why they were fighting in the first place. They decided to have a conciliatory meal, but a disagreement over who should pay resulted in a full scale brawl.

Things got even more manic in 'Internal Affairs', when another encounter between Peter and the Chicken resulted in thousands of their clones fighting, the man and bird clashing in space and the destruction of an oil rig. In the latest season we get the strangest chicken fight yet, as with time running backwards in 'Yug Ylimaf', we get to see a reverse battle between man and beast, which even involves them un-crashing a plane.

Sheldon The Turtle
From: 'Lois Comes Out Of her Shell'

Turtles are harmless, right? Well, it turns out they're not, as some of them can be very evil indeed. Stewie found Sheldon in a pond at the park and decided to take him home. After a close call with death, Stewie began to become suspicious that Sheldon was behind it. He flushed the turtle down the toilet, but the animal wasn't done with the baby, delivering teddy Rupert's decapitated head in a box to Stewie. Sheldon returns for a showdown with Stewie, resulting in a pitched battle. The youngest Griffin only survives because of the surprise appearance of videogame character Mario, who gets 100 points for jumping on and killing the turtle.

New Brian
From: 'The Man With Two Brians'

New Brian seemed like the perfect pet. When the Griffins decided to buy a new dog to replace the aging Brian, New Brian quickly won the family over by listening to Meg's problems, waking Peter & Lois with beautiful music and helping Chris with his homework. Stewie stayed loyal to the original Brian though (who had moved out due to the family trying to replace him) and told New Brian that everybody hated him. The new pooch responded by saying everyone loved him, especially Stewie's teddy Rupert, who New Brian had been humping. Stewie didn't take the news well, as he killed New Brian, chopped him up and put him in the garbage.

FAMILY GUY GOES TIME TRAVELLING

Family Guy loves a bit of time travel, from Peter being sent back to 1984, to Stewie, Brian and Mort ending up in Nazi Germany. We take a look at the show's temporal antics, as well as the machine Stewie built so that he can zip through history.

THE TIME MACHINE

Stewie's main time machine is a walk-in chamber you have to step into, dial up when you'd like to travel to, press the button and then you're zapped to whatever point in history you want.

The other key component is the return pad, which you power-up, step on and it zooms you back to the present. As you can't guarantee there'll be a power source in the past, Stewie initially gets the pad to run on radioactive uranium, a substance that's not always readily available. While it's an incredible invention, it can also cause a whole lot of trouble.

INTERNAL AFFAIRS
Season: 10

There's only a little bit of time travel in this one, but when it comes, it's good. During an epic fight with the Giant Chicken, Peter and the bird accidentally step onto Stewie's time pad, which sends them back to the Wild West in 1885. Once there they end up colliding with Marty McFly and the Delorean time machine from Back To The Future III, which allows them return to the present. They're so caught up in the fight, they don't even seem to realise they've travelled through time!

YUG YLIMAF
Season: 11

Brian uses the time machine as a way to impress women, but when he realises that Stewie will notice all the extra years he's added to the machine's clock, he decides to turn the dials back. That's a bad idea as it causes an explosion that results in time going backwards for everyone except Stewie and Brian. As they pass through events from earlier episodes of Family Guy, they realise that the reversal of time is speeding up, and that if they don't sort it out soon, Stewie will become unborn!

THE BIG BANG THEORY
Season: 9

Stewie comes up with a plan to get all the best jokes by going back in time and stealing other's lines before they get to say them. When Brian tries to stop this, they end up getting zapped outside time and space. The only way back is to cause an explosion, which Stewie soon realises is the Big Bang – he created the universe! When his arch-enemy half-brother, Bertram, notices Stewie shopping for parts to fix his time pad, he realises what the baby is up to, so he hijacks the machine and goes back to the renaissance so that he can kill Stewie's direct ancestor, Leonardo Da Vinci. If Da Vinci is murdered, Stewie will never exist!

BACK TO THE PILOT
Season: 10

Brian wishes that he could find a tennis ball he buried in the back garden years ago, so Stewie offers to take him back in his time machine so that the dog can see where he buried it. When they arrive in the past they end up taking a look in at the family, who are doing the things that happened in Family Guy's pilot episode. Stewie warns Brian not to interact with anyone, but the dog can't help himself. When they return to the present, it becomes clear Brian told his younger self about 9/11, and so the terrorist atrocity was prevented. They discover that perhaps this isn't as good as it first appears, when a massive world war breaks out.

ROAD TO GERMANY
Season: 7

The Griffins are holding an Oscar viewing party, but when Mort needs to use the bathroom in a hurry, he ends up going through the wrong door. When they can't find him anywhere, Stewie and Brian realise that Mort may have mistaken the baby's new time machine for a portable loo. As Mort has no way back to the present, they resolve to travel back in time to save him, ending up in Warsaw on September 1st, 1939. Initially they can't work out why that date sounds familiar, until they realise they're in the firing line on the day the Nazis invaded Poland. With the return pad broken, Mort, Brian and Stewie must travel to Britain and then into the heart of Berlin to get it working.

TIME TRAVELLING WITHOUT THE MACHINE

Stewie's walk-in machine isn't the only way Family guy has allowed the Griffins to travel through time. The baby's first time machine was a much smaller device in the episode 'Mind Over Murder', which he invented so that he could jump over the pain of teething.

However, when the plans for the machine were discovered, he was so worried about the breach of security he travelled back to before his plans were discovered. This turns out to be great timing, as the Griffin house was about to go up in flames..

Peter also has a time travel adventure in the episode 'Meet The Quagmires', although that time no machine was involved at all.

Instead Peter used the fact that Death has the ability to send people through time to allow him to go back to 1984, so he could experience single life again.

Death also allows Peter to see an alternate version of what his life would have been without alcohol in 'The Friends Of Peter G.', which is kind of like time travel, but through an alternate reality.

FAMILY GUY

WORD SEARCH

```
N I F F I R G S I O L I T T S N F R L W A P A R L N I M E
N T J P R P A S W Y Y I T G A T N E R E O B I S I A E E W
L O H R H W F A F R T S O I S C T G N C N S S I K M R J Y
E M T E U T T A A R E N G R R S W A O A R A E A W D A O N
T N M R G G M N I W R S S N A O N W S E E Y R G O L N Y C
A A A I U I O E L I T I P J W E L 5 N R D T C K B O E C A
S B F L L B A O N L R R A O A O G R A I I A T C E G O E A
P F E Y R A R N E E L W P S O J N R W K R C E Y A T O K O
I O G E S A K A T R O M U C W N R N S T K M O G W R C I I
E U R N C H F U W C O K I D C L E V E L A N D B R O W N N
Y N O R E B R C N K H N E C L M U R I E L G O L D M A N S
A W A N A K A T A I C I R T K I P R S W R N R N I E A E H
S N B I O O N T S M S I C T N E R C U T N G L Y A E O Y N
O J I F N R C A I D H N R K W H Y O S I R S H S G N J I W
M O A F I N I R G S G T S T E T C M E N L E N T N L E E O
W E N I A A S O H T I I E A A N E S C I N R E S E T S R R
L S G R E B G E L P H R A S N P W O K F O T K T S S S M B
K W L G V D R L D M S N K O M A N I F F I R G R E T E P A
S A F S R B I G U C D N O S N A W S E I N N O B G B L L T
F N H I E I F A H P O T R S C 5 I C C R G B N N B G S L T
Y S R R E A F M N I O M O N N E M L A G X N L I I Q A E E
O O T H T G I F A E W N A M D L O G L E I R U M U E W R
F N Y C A D N S I W S S A Y T R S I L I T U T E U A D S O
L I E O T T B I D N E I Y C O U W A A W W P A A C H N O L
J W T W C H M R O A M W M U N R C S L E N E I T N O I E Y
T M O R T G O L D M A N E M T R W K O T E R I U B G B J E
I O T M S E S O E C J S D W O O N E E S M T E L K C I W T
S E H G T H L N A C T I O N 5 N E W S R M E G S L R R F N
I A E B I S N R H L M N L O M O S S N T E E N M U O T A N
```

CAN YOU FIND ALL THE WORDS BELOW IN THE GRID?

- ★ ACTION 5 NEWS
- ★ ALEX BORSTEIN
- ★ CAROL WEST
- ★ CARTER PEWTERSCHMIDT
- ★ CHRIS GRIFFIN
- ★ CLEVELAND BROWN
- ★ DIANE SIMMONS
- ★ FAMILY GUY
- ★ FRANCIS GRIFFIN
- ★ GIANT CHICKEN
- ★ HERBERT
- ★ JAMES WOODS HIGH SCHOOL
- ★ JESSE
- ★ JOE SWANSON

- ★ JOYCE KINNEY
- ★ LOIS GRIFFIN
- ★ LORETTA BROWN
- ★ MAYOR WEST
- ★ MEG GRIFFIN
- ★ MICKEY MCFINNIGAN
- ★ MILA KUNIS
- ★ MORT GOLDMAN
- ★ MURIEL GOLDMAN
- ★ OLLIE WILLIAMS

- ★ PATRICK WARBURTON
- ★ PETER GRIFFIN
- ★ QUAHOG
- ★ RUPERT
- ★ SETH GREEN
- ★ SETH MACFARLANE
- ★ SPOONER STREET
- ★ STEWIE GRIFFIN
- ★ SUSIE SWANSON
- ★ TOM TUCKER
- ★ TRICIA TAKANAWA

FAMILY GUY
in love

Family Guy gets very romantic in Season 11 with the episode 'Valentine's Day In Quahog', which follows the love lives of various characters, from Meg getting her kidney stolen on a date, to Mayor West discovering his wife is seeing other mayors behind his back!

However, this isn't the shows' only flirtation with love, as over the years everyone's had some sort of romantic interest. We take a look back at Family Guy in love.

Peter & Lois

These two only have eyes for one another, don't they? Well, most of the time that's true, but in 'Bill and Peter's Bogus Journey' Lois ends up sleeping with Bill Clinton. Lois initially tries to save her marriage by allowing Peter to cheat with someone too (he chooses his wife's mom, Barbara), but Peter eventually realises Bill's incredibly persuasive when he also ends up in the ex-President's bed.

Meg

As with most things in her life, Meg isn't exactly lucky in love. In the early days of Family Guy, her only romantic option was Neil Goldman. However as Neil is even grosser than Meg, she constantly spurned him – and that's despite them once kissing when they thought they were about to die, as well as Meg being sold to Neil (via Mort) by Peter.

The boy she really wanted back then was Joe's son, Kevin, but she never got very far with him. She has had a few brief relationships

though, such as dating nudist Jeff Campbell, having ear sex with a boy called Doug and pretending she was a lesbian and dating a woman (just because the LGBT club made her feel included).

Her romances sometimes go way too far, such as when she dated a prisoner called Luke, as when she helped him escape, she ended up getting locked up too.

The only time she dated a normal person, in 'Go, Stewie, Go', Lois ended up seducing him.

Stewie

Stewie may be a baby, but that doesn't mean he can't have a romantic life, even if it is a little confused. Much of the time it seems he's gay, such as occasions when he's invited guys over to his hotel room, or when he's dressed as a woman called Desiree so he can go on dates with grown men. But then, it's not quite that simple, as he's also shown inappropriate interest in Brian, as well as having fantasies where his stuffed toy Rupert has a muscular man's body, but still with a teddy's head. That's not to say he has no interest in women though, as several times he's had a crush on a female toddler. For example, in 'Dammit Janet!' he falls for a girl in his daycare but turns on her when he realises she doesn't like him, she just wants a cookie. Another time he vowed to turn the gutter-mouthed British toddler, Eliza Pinchley, into a lady, realising by the end of the experience that he was madly in love with her.

He also thought he'd found his soulmate in the form of Penelope, as she was a genius with an evil streak as big as Stewie, but they eventually fell out when she demanded that he kill Brian!

Chris

The eldest Griffin boy has had slightly better luck in love than his sister, but not by much! perhaps it would be better if Chris didn't date at all, as in 'Love Thy Trophy' he says that he thinks babies come from the child welfare office!

One of his first romances caused him a bit of confusion over his sexuality, as when the Griffins were staying in the town of Bumblescum, he befriended someone called Sam, who ended up kissing him. Chris got more than a little confused, but eventually explained that he only likes women, at which point Sam revealed that she was a girl but just likes wearing tomboy clothing.

Much of the time he's very shy around girls, but that's not always a bad thing, as when he plucks up courage to ask out Ellen, who has Down Syndrome, he discovers that she's very high maintenance. He was a little too successful in love in the episode 'Jungle Love'. In that instalment Chris ran away to the Amazon and accidentally ended up getting married to a young girl called Loka.

Brian

None of the Griffins is as obsessed with their love life as much as Brian is, who can often be found bemoaning the fact that he can never keep a woman. However, while he talks about wanting a woman who shares his interests, he generally goes for dim blondes. There's been a long line of these, but none like Jillian, who was dumb as a box of rocks but who truly loved Brian. The dog broke her heart though and she married someone else. Nevertheless, Brian has said she's his soulmate.

His need for dumb women was proved when he dated reality TV star Lauren Conrad, who was far smarter than Brian and patronised him in the same way he normally patronised his dates. Brian hated suddenly be the stupid one in the relationship (their romance ended because he gave Lauren worms). Few of his other relationships have lasted long, often because of his lies. For example, when he dated the blind Kate, who hated dogs, he pretended he wasn't a pooch. Brian also has a bit of a thing for older women, having romanced the elderly Pear Burton just before she died, as well as dating the 50-something Rita. There's one brief liaison with a slightly older lady that Brian will certainly never forget. He slept with Ida, who turned out to be Quagmire's father who'd had a sex change operation.

QUAGMIRE'S CONQUESTS

It would be fair to describe Glenn Quagmire as a pervert, but as he's slept with at least 600 women he certainly knows how to get ladies into the sack. So how does he do so well? Here's our guide on being as much of a sex hound as Glenn Quagmire.

welcome to the adult club

GiGGiTY!

---

1. TURN YOUR HOUSE INTO A MAGNIFICENT SEX PALACE

You need to be prepared, as there's nothing worse than bringing a woman home and then having to kill the mood while you run around getting everything ready. Glenn has this covered, as at the touch of a button his entire house converts from a normal abode to a temple of sexual pleasure. Various surfaces revolve or slide out to become beds, while all manner of sexual devices swing into place.

It's also a good idea to have plenty of toys. Glenn has slings, ball gags, whips, and all manner of other things, which ensure that he can take part in any sort of congress that comes his way.

2. FIND THE RIGHT LADIES & BE THE RIGHT TYPE OF GUY FOR THEM

The sentence above might make it sound like you have to act like a good person and find an angelic woman, but what Quagmire advocates is pretty much the opposite. Glenn is so good at picking up the chicks that he even teaches a class in it but, as he points out to Brian, it's not just about the chat-up lines and moves, it's also about targeting the right woman (preferably needy and slightly damaged) in the right way to get into their pants. Brian fails at the class because he's looking for love, but Glenn says that doesn't matter, it's just about looking for women who are desperate enough and then moving in with the right line. As he says, "This course is in getting laid, not finding love."

3. DON'T GET PUT OFF AND DON'T BE PICKY

Even a veteran sex hound is probably going to strike out more than he scores, but Glenn never lets this get to him. If a line doesn't work on a woman, he just shakes it off and moves onto the next one. Glenn's been knocked back so much and so hard that he's developed an immunity to pepper spray. He'll literally chat up one woman after another, such as hitting on three chicks in the space of ten seconds with lines like "Hey baby, if I could rearrange the alphabet, I'd put U and I together", "Hey, are you a parking ticket? 'Cause you've got 'fine# written all over you," and (to two women) "Hey, I don't wanna come between you.....or do I?" The first women to say "yes" is the winner and you take her home (or go wherever she'll agree to do it)

4. FIND THE PLACES YOU'RE MOST LIKELY TO SCORE

If all you want to do is have sex, it's not just about going to the obvious places to find partners – after all, in a bar there may be plenty of women, but you've also got a lot of other guys trying to get with them. One of the things Quagmire has perfected is finding those places where his likelihood of having sex is much higher than average. For example he knows numerous women in prison, so that he can go and have conjugal visits with them (as he says, he likes to do women in the can). If you do have to go somewhere where you'll face more competition, you can increase your chances by getting friendly with the staff. There's one place Glenn goes that'll serve him a 'roofie colada', so that he can drug a potential conquest.

5. DON'T RULE ANYTHING OUT

You may have morals and limits about what you will and won't have sex with, but if you want to bang as many people as Glenn, you need to put those aside. Animals aren't out of the question, such as when Quagmire woke one morning being nuzzled by a giraffe. He wasn't freaked by having the animal there, he wigged out because it was a different one from the night before! He also attempted to set up a threesome between himself, his mother and a woman from the reality show, The Bachelorette. Glenn doesn't usually have sex with men, but did once have sex with Joe, thinking that he was a woman, and he doesn't mind if someone was born male but has finished their sex change – even if he's not that comfortable with his own father having transitioned into a woman.

6. DON'T GO TOO FAR!

There are a few things that Quagmire does that we really can't recommend (not least the roofie colada mentioned above). For example, when someone crashes into Quagmire's garage, it allows a hoard of scantily class Asian sex slaves to escape. It may guarantee sex, but buying sex slaves is really going too far. Having sex with the family of friends isn't a good idea either, as Glenn destroyed Cleveland's marriage by sleeping with Loretta and almost ruined his friendship with Peter by hitting on Meg the moment she turned 18. Glenn has also occasionally suggested an affinity for necrophilia and loves unprotected sex so much that he has nearly every disease imaginable. And also unlike Glenn, if a woman doesn't want to sleep with you, don't force it!

GIGGITY!
GIGGITY!

FAMILY GUY

Boardgame

DO PEOPLE IN OTHER CASTLES

THINK THIS IS FUNNY?

The aim of the game is to get from the start spot to the win square.

Each player takes it in turns to throw the dice, and then moves forward the number of squares they've thrown.

Follow the instructions on the square you land on (if there are any).

You will need:

- A dice
- Enough counters for every player

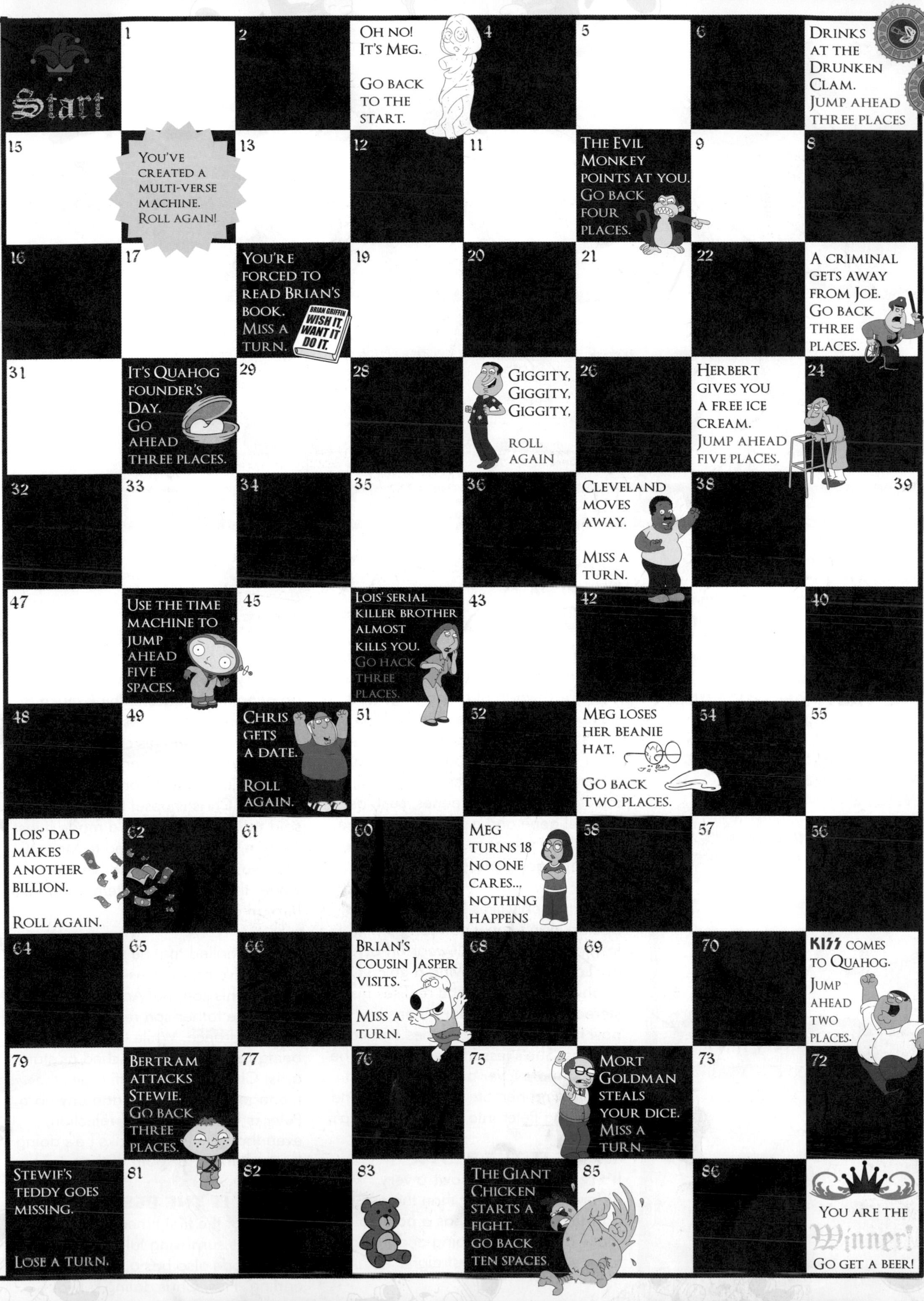

Start

| 1 | 2 | OH NO! IT'S MEG. GO BACK TO THE START. | 4 | 5 | 6 | DRINKS AT THE DRUNKEN CLAM. JUMP AHEAD THREE PLACES |

15 | YOU'VE CREATED A MULTI-VERSE MACHINE. ROLL AGAIN! | 13 | 12 | 11 | THE EVIL MONKEY POINTS AT YOU. GO BACK FOUR PLACES. | 9 | 8

16 | 17 | YOU'RE FORCED TO READ BRIAN'S BOOK. MISS A TURN. | 19 | 20 | 21 | 22 | A CRIMINAL GETS AWAY FROM JOE. GO BACK THREE PLACES.

31 | IT'S QUAHOG FOUNDER'S DAY. GO AHEAD THREE PLACES. | 29 | 28 | GIGGITY, GIGGITY, GIGGITY, ROLL AGAIN | 26 | HERBERT GIVES YOU A FREE ICE CREAM. JUMP AHEAD FIVE PLACES. | 24

32 | 33 | 34 | 35 | 36 | CLEVELAND MOVES AWAY. MISS A TURN. | 38 | 39

47 | USE THE TIME MACHINE TO JUMP AHEAD FIVE SPACES. | 45 | LOIS' SERIAL KILLER BROTHER ALMOST KILLS YOU. GO BACK THREE PLACES. | 43 | 42 | 40

48 | 49 | CHRIS GETS A DATE. ROLL AGAIN. | 51 | 52 | MEG LOSES HER BEANIE HAT. GO BACK TWO PLACES. | 54 | 55

LOIS' DAD MAKES ANOTHER BILLION. ROLL AGAIN. | 62 | 61 | 60 | MEG TURNS 18 NO ONE CARES... NOTHING HAPPENS | 58 | 57 | 56

64 | 65 | 66 | BRIAN'S COUSIN JASPER VISITS. MISS A TURN. | 68 | 69 | 70 | KISS COMES TO QUAHOG. JUMP AHEAD TWO PLACES.

79 | BERTRAM ATTACKS STEWIE. GO BACK THREE PLACES. | 77 | 76 | 75 | MORT GOLDMAN STEALS YOUR DICE. MISS A TURN. | 73 | 72

STEWIE'S TEDDY GOES MISSING. LOSE A TURN. | 81 | 82 | 83 | THE GIANT CHICKEN STARTS A FIGHT. GO BACK TEN SPACES. | 85 | 86 | YOU ARE THE Winner! GO GET A BEER!

71

200 EPISODES LATER...

EACH CHARACTER'S TOP FAMILY GUY EPISODE

WITH OVER 200 EPISODES OF FAMILY GUY TO CHOOSE FROM, IT'S TOUGH TO PICK OUT JUST 10 AS THE BEST EVER. HOWEVER, WE'VE RUMBLED THROUGH THE VAULT AND PICKED OUT THE BEST EPS. FEATURING EACH OF THE MAIN CHARACTERS, AND THE BEST WITH THE WHOLE FAMILY.

TAKE A LOOK AND SEE IF YOU AGREE WITH THESE PICKS...

BEST PETER EPISODE
Family Gay
Season 7

WHAT'S IT ABOUT?: Peter buys a brain-damaged horse, which causes $100,000 worth of damage when it goes on the rampage. The Griffins don't have that kind of cash, so Peter agrees to take part in medical experiments for money. He gets injected with various genes, such as a squirrel gene and a Seth Rogen gene. Everything seems to go okay until he's given the gay gene.

Peter now only likes men and the doctors don't know how long it might last, or indeed if it will wear off at all. Lois' horror at having a gay hubby lessens when she realises his stereotypical behaviour means he now likes to shop for clothes and cook muffins. She's less impressed when he takes a male lover and tells Lois that he's leaving her. Stewie and Brian end up forcing Peter into a 'straight camp'.

WHY'S IT THE BEST?:
It's very funny and shows a very different side to Peter than the one we normally see. It also has a point to make about stereotyping and trying to force someone to be straight.

BEST CHRIS EPISODE
A Picture's Worth A 1,000 Bucks
Season 2

WHAT'S IT ABOUT?: On Peter's birthday, Chris gives his father a painting. Peter doesn't think much of his gift and simply uses it to cover a broken window in his car. This allows art dealer Antonio Monatti to see the painting and buy it from Peter for $5,000. Chris is upset that his dad sold the painting, as he'd made it just for him, but Peter's talked to Monatti, who wants Chris to go to New York where the dealer will attempt to make him an art sensation.

Peter is thrilled that he's going to be able to live his dreams vicariously through his son, but Antonio starts to see the father-son relationship as a hindrance. While Chris is being restyled and launched as star artist Christobel, Monatti urges the teenager not to see his dad anymore. Peter is furious at Chris' rejection, even though his son thinks he's doing the best thing for both of them.

WHY'S IT THE BEST?:
It's one of the first times we see that Chris has surprising talents, and the episode also has a rather sweet ending. Plus, Chris dating a two-dimensional Kate Moss is very funny.

BEST MEG EPISODE
Prick up Your Ears
Season 5

WHAT'S IT ABOUT?: A miracle has happened – Meg has got herself a boyfriend, and he seems completely normal! Meg is enjoying her new relationship with Jerry when, as usual, her family make things more difficult. Lois becomes the school's sex-ed teacher, but quickly gets fired when some parents discover she's teaching the kids about condoms, rather than scaring them off sex altogether. Instead the school hires the Christian group, The Opal Ring Crusade, who tell all the kids they must be abstinent.

Meg and Jerry get caught up in the school's enthusiasm for abstinence. They both vow not to have normal sex and instead engage in something they don't think counts – ear sex – which allows them to be intimate without properly 'doing it'. Lois catches Meg and her boyfriend engaging in this 'unnatural' congress and so decides to have a word with her daughter to convince her real sex is better. However, when Meg and Jerry decide that perhaps abstinence isn't right for them, it doesn't turn out well for the Griffin girl, as her boyfriend leaves her after he sees her naked.

WHY'S IT THE BEST?:
It's an episode that pretty much sums Meg up – desperate for a boyfriend, wanting to fit in and open to any craze that sweeps the school. We wouldn't advise trying ear sex though.

BEST STEWIE EPISODE
Emission Impossible
Season 3

WHAT'S IT ABOUT?: Peter and Lois go to see her pregnant sister Carol, which results in Peter acting as midwife when Carol goes into labour. The experience makes Lois broody and she decides she wants another child, which Peter agrees to. When they tell the family, Stewie isn't impressed about the idea of being usurped as the youngest in the family, and so vows to stop Lois and Peter conceiving.

Stewie initially attempts to stop his parents from having sex at all, such as crying for attention, smearing lipstick on Peter's collar and building a Peter robot that insults Lois. When these don't work, he decides there's nothing for it but to use his miniaturisation device to make himself small enough to fly inside Peter's body and destroy all his sperm. Once he's piloted to Peter's testicles he set about his destructive job, but gets more than he bargained for when he meets an evil-genius-sperm who wants to be born – Bertram.

WHY'S IT THE BEST?:
There's action, plenty of laughs and one of Stewie's best inventions – the miniaturisation device. Plus we get to meet the malevolent but funny Bertram for the first time. What's not to like?

BEST LOIS EPISODE
Model Misbehavior
Season 4

WHAT'S IT ABOUT?: While visiting her parents, Lois reminisces about how she had aspirations of being a model, which her father crushed. Even though her dad is still against it, she decides to get work as a model and soon starts to find success. Initially Peter is thrilled to have a hot model as a wife, but begins to get very jealous when he sees how other guys lust after her.

Lois rebels against Peter's disapproval, as he seems to be doing exactly what her father did. She begins taking diet pills so she can get as unhealthily skinny as the other models (until she can play her ribs like a xylophone) and cares far more for her looks than her health or family. Peter teams up with Carter to get Lois out of modelling. They're going kidnap her at a Vogue party and take her home.

WHY'S IT THE BEST?:
Lois is best when we get to see her taking things to the extreme. While normally so normal and conservative, when she rebels she really goes all out!

BEST BRIAN EPISODE
Brian Wallows and Peter Swallows
Season 3

WHAT'S IT ABOUT?: After drowning his sorrows over the state of his love life, Brian gets pulled over for drink driving and is sentenced to do community service. He's sent to the 'Outreach to the Elderly' program and assigned to help a mean-tempered, elderly shut-in called Pearl Burton. Pearl constantly criticises everything Brian does, and if there isn't anything to criticise, she invents something. Eventually Brian can't take anymore and storms out.

While watching TV, Brian happens upon a programme about a woman who sang jingles for commercials, but her attempt to be taken seriously as an artiste fell flat when she was heckled at Carnegie Hall, even though her singing was beautiful. Brian realises the woman was Pearl! He goes back to her house to tell her he loved her performance all those decades ago, and hopes to convince her to leave her house for the first time in years.

WHY'S IT THE BEST?:
Sometimes Family Guy is good at creating plots that touch you emotionally by the end, and this is one such episode – even if it is about a sort-of romance between an old lady and a dog.

BEST CLEVELAND EPISODE
The Cleveland-Loretta Quagmire
Season 4

WHAT'S IT ABOUT?: During a party at sea on Peter's fishing boat, a fish lands in Cleveland's wife Loretta's cleavage and she invites Quagmire to get it out. Cleveland doesn't seem that bothered about his wife's flirting though. Later on Peter hears screams coming from Cleveland's house. Brian and Peter rush in to see Loretta having sex with a man who has a tattoo on his bum, but they don't see who it is – we do though, it's Quagmire. The dog and his master tell Lois, the Swansons and Quagmire about Loretta cheating, with Peter saying that he'll break the news to Cleveland.

When Cleveland confronts Loretta, she says she needs a real man. After Cleveland only gives a very mild-mannered response to this, Loretta kicks him out. Cleveland ends up staying with the Griffins but he doesn't seem too affected by the breakdown of his marriage. He's not even shocked when he discovers it was Quagmire who slept with his wife. But Cleveland's easy-going manner can't last forever.

WHY'S IT THE BEST?: This was one of those game-changer episodes, as it was the end of Cleveland's marriage forever. It also explored Cleveland's personality like no other episode, showing how mild he is – until he's pushed too far.

BEST JOE EPISODE
Believe It or Not, Joe's Walking on Air
Season 6

WHAT'S IT ABOUT?: Peter builds a men's club in his backyard so that he and his friends can hang out without any women around. Their wives aren't impressed with this and so decide to muscle in. Joe gets upset when all the women are dancing except for his wife. Bonnie says she's fine just sitting with him, because he's disabled. Not long afterwards Joe hears about a revolutionary new surgery that might allow him to walk again – a leg transplant.

He gets one and a few weeks later he's strolling out of hospital on his own two feet. Joe immediately sets out to do everything he couldn't do when he was in a wheelchair, such as taking part in a musical number and practicing karate. He soon starts to get fed up with Peter, Cleveland, and Quagmire, deciding they're lazy and that he only hung out with them because he was crippled. He finds new friends and even decides to leave Bonnie. With Joe getting out of hand, all those from his old life decide there's no other option but to paralyse Joe again!

WHY'S IT THE BEST?: It's always good to see a character in a different light and that's certainly true here, where we learn Joe might actually be a better person because he's in a wheelchair.

BEST QUAGMIRE EPISODE
Meet The Quagmires
Season 5

WHAT'S IT ABOUT?: Peter feels like he's missed out after he hears all about Quagmire's sexual exploits, so he summons Death and asks if he and Brian can be sent back to 1984 for a night, so that Peter can be single again. Once he's back in the past, Peter cancels the date he was supposed to have with Lois so that he can go dancing with a young Cleveland. It's a great night and he even ends up making out with 80s star Molly Ringwald.

The next day he's back in the present, but quickly realises that what he did in the past has drastically altered the present. He's now been married to Molly Ringwald for 20 years! He discovers that Lois isn't too far away, as she's married to Quagmire and loves her hubby's sex-hound antics. Lois and Glenn also have three children, who look like Meg, Chris and Stewie but with Quagmire's chin and tendency to say 'giggity'. Peter begs death to send him back to 1984 again to see if he can undo the damage he's done.

WHY'S IT THE BEST?:
While technically this is more about Peter than Quagmire, it's Glenn's best episode simply for the image of Meg, Chris and Stewie as his children.

BEST GRIFFIN FAMILY EPISODE
Peter Peter Caviar Eater
Season 2

WHAT'S IT ABOUT?: Lois' filthy rich aunt Marguerite Pewterschmidt comes to visit, but drops dead on their doorstep. It turns out that's good for the Griffins, as she has left her palatial Newport, Rhode Island mansion, Cherrywood Manor, to Lois. The family head off to take a look, getting a warm, musical greeting from the staff. Right afterwards all the staff start to leave, as they say they were only paid up to the song, but Peter hires them back, telling them he's got the cash to pay them from selling the family home in Quahog.

Peter has difficulty fitting into his new blueblood life, so he begs Brian to teach him how to be a gentleman. The usual techniques don't work until Brian tries shock therapy, which works a little too well, making Peter convinced he really is a multi-millionaire. Stewie meanwhile is enjoying bossing servants around, and Lois isn't sure she wants to return to a life of wealth.

WHY'S IT THE BEST?: We learn a lot about the family in this episode, such as Lois' wealthy background (it's the first time we see her rich parents), as well as that Peter's middle name is Lowenbrau. Plus it's got the wonderful song, 'This House Is Freakin' Sweet'.

GOODBYE FROM
SPOONER STREET

We've had a lot of fun with the Griffins, but now it's time to say goodbye. Don't worry though, Quahog's finest (or should that be most notorious?) will be back with more nutty madness soon.

It's certainly been a crazy year, with the Griffins heading to the top of Mount Everest, Stewie becoming unborn, the family going into space, Quagmire accidentally getting married (again) and Stewie getting embroiled in a battle with an evil turtle. We even got the strangest love triangle ever when Peter fell in love with a phone sex worker, without realising it was actually his wife Lois!

We'll also have to ponder whether it was really a good idea for Chris to movie in with Herbert, or if Carter should have hidden the cure for cancer away from the world for many years.

If all that happened in one season, who knows what they'll get up to next? So until next time, it's farewell from Peter, Lois, Meg, Chris, Stewie, Brian, Joe, Quagmire and the rest of the gang.

"YUG YLIMAF"

"LOIS COMES OUT OF HER SHELL"

"THE GIGGITY WIFE"

"CHRIS CROSS"

"CALL GIRL"

"INTO FAT AIR"

"THE OLD MAN AND THE BIG 'C'"

ANSWERS

PAGES 28-29

1. The Super Bowl
2. 1999
3. Spooner Street
4. Virginia
5. Loretta
6. Cross
7. Lando Griffin
8. Nate Griffin
9. Dawson's Creek
10. Lois
11. Peter
12. Gears
13. Drug sniffing dog
14. Happy-Go-Lucky Toy Company
15. Jonathan Weed
16. Bumblescum
17. The Campbells
18. PTV
19. South America
20. New England Patriots
21. The London Sillinannies
22. Joan
23. Peterotica
24. Dingo And The Baby
25. Ireland
26. Bill Clinton
27. Because the people of Quahog think he's possessed by the Devil
28. Molly Ringwald
29. He had a stroke
30. By using stem cells
31. Dylan
32. Jesus
33. New Brian
34. Stewie kills him
35. He temporarily becomes gay
36. Misery
37. Bitch Stewie
38. Ellen
39. Dan
40. Ida
41. Pink
42. Dr. Hartman
43. Herbert
44. Leonardo Da Vinci
45. Hurricane Flozell
46. He's a dolphin
47. Ricky Gervais
48. Saggy Naggy
49. Death Has A Shadow
50. 'The Life of Larry' and 'Larry & Steve'

PAGES 54-55

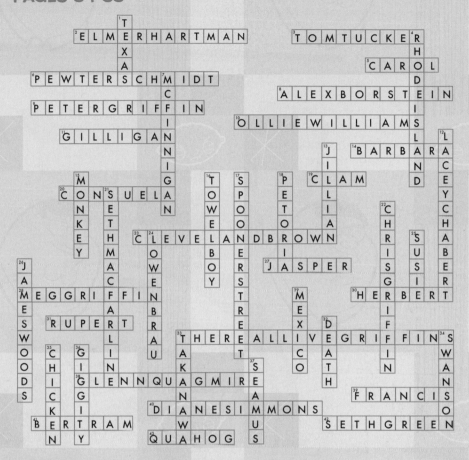

PAGES 64-65

Family Guy Annual 2014

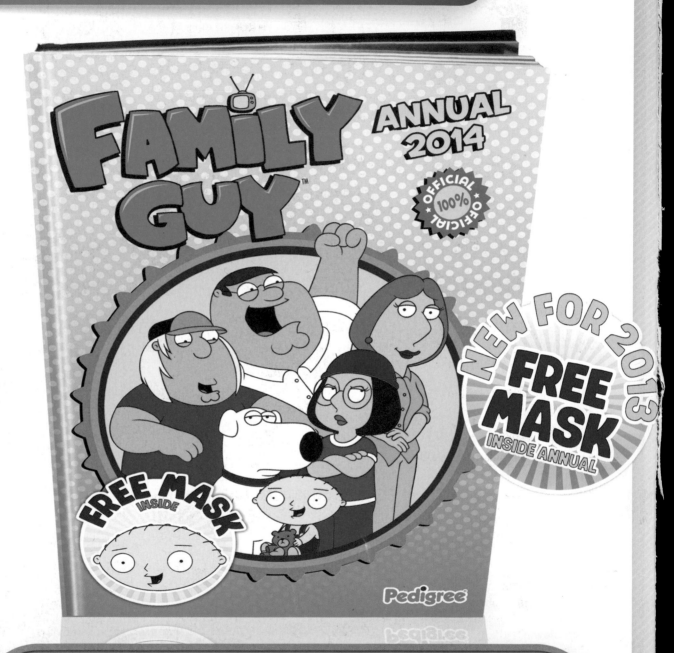

Visit www.pedigreebooks.com

Pedigree Books, Beech Hill House, Walnut Gardens, Exeter EX4 4DH